Wishing You a joyful reading. I am deeply honored that you chose to pick up my book among so many others. I hope these pages offer you something valuable. Your support keeps me inspired to write more. Happy reading!

Dr. Shivakumar G S

EDUCATIONAL TECHNOLOGY
VOLUME-I

By
Dr. Shivakumar G S
Principal
Kumadvathi College of Education,
Shikaripura, Shivamogga-District
Karnataka
India

Made with ♥ on the Notion Press Platform
www.notionpress.com

PREFACE

Educational technology is a course of study that examines the method of investigating, planning, developing, executing, and judging the instructional context and learning elements to enhance teaching and education. The main purpose of educational technology or instructional technology is to strengthen education. Technology in education helps in learning the subject with a better understanding.

Educational technology helps in resolving school problems that involve motivation, and skills like analytical, problem solving etc. With the advancement of educational technologies, books are converted into eBooks. Lessons are now animated for a clear understanding of topics, clearing the doubts digitally when compared to the previous method of teaching. Students now have unlimited resources for learning only because of educational technology. Blackboard became a digital board, Classes became online, students are now taught on LCD projectors and the list grows on.

Educators in public schools and faculty at universities need to know what types of materials are available, how to use them, why and when they should be used, and how to combine them into the instruction/education background to meet the final goal of developing the education. Coaches also need to solemnly examine how these modern materials can affect what we learn and teach. Technology can be used for knowledge-based training procedures or it can be used to implement a student self-development approach. Educators need to know how technology can transform education. Teaching how to use technology will begin to improve the educational system. India has seen drastic Edtech startups in the last 4 years that are bringing revolutions in educational technologies and breaking the barrier, this is helping in shaping future generations with better skills by teaching them visual lessons and the latest information.

Dr. Shivakumar G S

ACKNOWLEDGEMENTS

The author expresses his most sincere and heartfelt gratitude to the Secretary, Director, and President of Swamy Vivekananda Vidyasamsthe Trust, Shikaripura as well other Management body for their wholehearted support and cooperation in the successful completion of this work. The author expresses his sincere thanks to his wife Smt, Usha. M.S., whose painstaking efforts have enabled this work well in time. I express my deep gratitude to my parents Sri. M.G.Siddabasappa and Smt.Gangamma, G.P, and daughter Shravaya, G.S and Shreshta, G.S for their cooperation, encouragement, and help. Finally, I thank all my colleagues and friends for their constant concern and encouragement.

Dr. Shivakumar G S

TABLE OF CONTENTS

UNIT-1: EDUCATIONAL TECHNOLOGY

1.1 Meaning and objectives of educational technology.

Introduction:

Educational technology (commonly abbreviated as **edutech** or **edtech**) is the combined use of computer hardware, software, and educational theory and practice to facilitate learning. In addition to the practical educational experience, educational technology is based on theoretical knowledge from various disciplines such as communication, education, psychology, sociology, artificial intelligence, and computer science. It encompasses several domains including learning theory, computer-based training, online learning, and m-learning where mobile technologies are used.

Educational technology is a systematic application of relevant technological processes and resources in teaching, with a goal to improve students' performance. It involves a disciplined approach to identifying the needs of students, applying technology in instructions, and tracking their performance. A thickly populated country like India where mass education is the demand of the time, only educational technology is advisable. Software programme like programmed learning material can make mass education easily available. According to the intellectual level of the learner different programmed material like linear, branching, mathematics can be applied. Almost all types of courses considering the age level of the student can be programmed. Educational Technology possesses great potential for teaching learning process. It makes curriculum construction and selection of teaching learning strategies easy and also makes teaching-learning more effective.

Educational Technology helps in improving quality of teaching by providing varied types of programmes through TV and other media. Educational Technology motivates children for learning. It augments motivation among the learner to learn by using various new machines such as video, computer tape recorder, TV, and other different types of projected aid.

Educational technology almost eliminating the obstacles of mass instruction. Different types of programmes developed by different experts for a large population of students can be easily communicated educational opportunities accessible for all: It breaks the barrier of all classes of learners, irrespective of economic, social or geographical stat as and makes education available for all. For example, through mass media, TV, Radio, Film etc., it makes education easily available for all. It also serves as distance mode of learning.

Education Technology makes provision for self-instructional materials, which provide opportunities to both the gifted and backward children to proceed at his own rate of speed in the learning process.

Meaning of Educational Technology

The word "Technology" is derived from the two Greek words namely *Technic and Logia*. "Technic" -means art or skill. "Logia"- means Science or Study. So simplest meaning of "Technology" is "Science of study of an art or skill."

Definitions of Technology

"Technology is Knowledge organized for Production". - Sachs.I

"Technology is the application of scientific knowledge to a practical purpose". - Page.T "Technology is the set of instruments and skills which are used to satisfy the needs of the community". - Hierra. A.

Meaning of Education

The word "Education" is derived from the Latin word "Educatum", which means "To bring out". In the sense, the meaning of Education is to bring out the better qualities of the individual.

Acc. to Ross, the word "Education" is derived from the Latin word "Educare" which means "to bring up" or "to raise". It means that education is that process which brings up or rears the individual in the right way.

Meaning of Educational Technology

There are three views regarding the meaning of educational technology.

Educational Technology 1 (ET 1)

The first view which may call Educational Technology 1 (ET 1) refers to the application of physical sciences and engineering technology to provide mechanical instruments or "hardware" which can be used for instructional purposes. This is the view of James O. Finn and others (1960). E.g. Tape-recorders (including language laboratory), television, teaching machines and computer- based teaching.

Educational Technology 2 (ET 2)

The second view which we may call Educational Technology 2 (ET 2) refers to the application of scientific principles or „software approach" to instruction. This is the view of Skinner, Gagne and others.

Educational Technology 3 (ET 3)

The third and the modern view of Educational Technology 3 (ET 3) as described by Davis and Hartley (1972), incorporates both ET 1 and ET 2 through the application of a 'system approach" to education and training.

Definitions of Educational Technology

"Educational technology may be defined as the application of the laws as well as recent discoveries of science and technology to the process of education". - *S.S. Kulkarni* "Educational technology is the application of scientific process to man's learning conditions". - *Robert A. Cox*

"Educational technology is an application of scientific knowledge about learning to practical learning situation." - *J. Bloomer*

Characteristics of Educational Technology

1. ET has contributed in developing various methods e.g. Microteaching method, Interaction analysis, Audio Visual Aids and Programmed learning method.
2. In the field of ET, Psychology, Science and technology, system, art, AV aids and machines are used.
3. It is based on the application of the scientific knowledge.
4. It is helpful in making the teaching process objective, easy, clear, interesting and scientific. 5. It is a continuous dynamic technology.

6. It is an important medium of communication.
7. A desired change is possible in the behaviour of teachers and students

TECHNOLOGY OF EDUCATION AND TECHNOLOGY IN EDUCATION

Introduction

The term technology in education is a service concept like technology in the service of agriculture of farmers or science in the service of mankind. It refers to the use of equipment and machines for educational purposes. It involves the use of a wide range of audio- visual equipment's, hardware and sophisticated electronic devices like films, projectors, radio, television, tape recorder, teaching machines and computers etc.

Educational technology as explained earlier is a wider term than technology in education. It includes hardware approach, software approach and systems approach.

Educational Technology is broadly classified into the following two heads:

1. Technology of Education.
2. Technology in Education.

1. Technology of Education:

It is inherent in education itself. It refers to the application of behavioural sciences like psychology of educational theories and practical teaching –learning problems, instruction and motivation etc. It is concerned with the study of educational problems and the techniques to be used in solving the teaching-learning problems so that best results should be achieved. Broadly speaking, technologies of planning, financing and administration are also covered under the concept of technology of education. Techniques of curriculum planning, transacting and evaluating also come under technology of education. In technology of education, we use derived from psychology of learning. In general, following techniques are included in technology of education:

1. Analysis of instructional problems.
2. Selection of instruments for evaluation

3. Selection of strategies to obtain desired result from the teaching-learning process.
4. Teacher behaviour.
5. Programmed learning.
6. System analysis.

2. Technology in Education

Broadly speaking, technology in education implies the use of implements, tools and machines in education in the same manner as we use these for the development of agriculture and gardening and industry and in fact our everyday life to reap the fruit of scientific and technological developments. Under technology in education, we include electronic media projector, film, radio, T.V, teaching machine, computer and internet etc. Technology in education refers to the application of engineering principles and technology in the process of education. Basically, it is called hardware technology.

Silverman (1968) called this type of educational technology as "Relative Technology" and technology of education as "Constructive Educational Technology".

Differences between Technology of Education and Technology in Education

Areas	Technology of education	Technology in education
1. Basis	It is based on child psychology (age, ability and mental level).	It is based on the principles of physical sciences or engineering sciences.
2. Approach	Its approach is identified as software approach.	Its approach is identified as hardware approach.
3.Origin	Its origin lies in the application of behavioural sciences to the problems	Its origin lies in the application of physical sciences or engineering to education.

4.Examples	Text books, work books, newspaper etc.	TV, Radio, Slide Projector, Computer, OHP etc
5.Relation	It is related to learning aids.	It is related to teaching aids.
6.Requirement	The use of this approach does not require skilled personnel as in hardware technology.	Skilled personnel in hardware technology are needed.
7.Flexibility	This approach is very flexible	This approach is relatively rigid.
8.Type	It is called constructive educational technology	It is called relative technology
9.contribution to educational system	This approach is very helpful in understanding the need of the learners and educating them accordingly.	It is useful in mass education programmes.
10. Cost	It is less costly.	It is expensive.

NEED AND IMPORTANCE OF EDUCATIONAL TECHNOLOGY

Use of ET is needed in the process of education because of following reasons.

1. Population Explosion
   - Populations of Asian countries are increasing at a very fast speed and we cannot educate all these people just by using teachers in the class.
   - Modern media of communication like TV, Internet and CDs etc. can impart education to millions of people together in one setting.
2. Fast Generation of New knowledge

• New knowledge is expanding at a very fast speed.

• It is almost doubling in just 3 years.

• A teacher is not supposed to impart this huge amount of knowledge by tutorial or classroom teaching.

• ET can perform this function very easily.

3. Development of new strategies

   • It is the ET that has helped to develops new strategies in the field of education like, i. Microteaching (inculcation of teaching skills among teachers),

   ii. Programmed instruction (Preparation of instructional materials in written or CAI forms for individualized learning).

   iii. Instructional analysis (analysis of teaching materials into convenient parts to be presented to students one by one) and use of hardware technology in education etc.

4. Controlled Atmosphere

   • Education cannot be treated as plaything by some teachers after the introduction of ET.

   • It has made the whole process of teaching objective, clear, scientific and interesting. • The teacher controls the classroom environment in his own favour but his performance is evaluated simultaneously by applying tests.

5. Importance of Teacher's role

   • It emphasizes theories & Principles of teaching more than those of learning.

   • Thus, it has removed many of the defects of ET and has raised the significance & relevance of a teacher in the class.

6. Mass extension of Model teaching

   • The facilities of radio television and interest are new available of a large scale.

   • By demonstrating the effective teaching of renowned teachers on these media we can benefit millions of students together.

- Even the less effective and less skilled teachers can take the benefit of these demonstrations & improve their teaching. 7. Advantages to private students
- Many universities have given permission to students for private examinations, even in higher education.
- These students do not attend classes
- In order to maintain standard of education in higher education, the use of ET becomes a necessity.

8. Beneficial for teacher training colleges

- Even teacher training colleges cannot produce good teachers without the use of ET. • It is because; this branch of education puts emphasis on the modification of teacher"s behaviour. (E.g.) we can develop teaching skills in student with the help of microteaching techniques.

9. Improvement of school Administration

- ET helps us to analyze the problems of school administration scientifically leading to improvement in the system.
- This is done by applying various combinations of inputs or adopting the procedure followed by the other school systems.

10. Preservation of knowledge

- By using hardware technology, we can preserve knowledge in audio and video cassettes, CDs & floppy disks (Pen drive)

11. Development of teaching models

- When a definite combination of inputs and strategies gives good result repeatedly in a number of class room situations.
- It can be translated into teaching models to be used universally.
- It can be also led to the development of teaching theories.

12. Creation of Interesting learning situations

• ET can transform the teaching-learning process from burden to enjoy which, psychologically very sound for students. (e.g.) use of material aids in teaching increases the interest of students.

UTILITY / USE OF EDUCATIONAL TECHNOLOGY FOR TEACHERS

1. It has provided scientific and systematic approach to teachers to conduct action research in the classroom situations to overcome the classroom problems related to classroom environment, content, curriculum etc.
2. It helps the teacher to modernize and mechanize the teaching-learning process. It also helps the learners to study at their own speed/rate with the help of programmed instruction on video or computers.
3. ET supplements the teacher, with AV-aids to make the teaching-learning process more effective.
4. It helps in teacher's professional growth.
5. Add to their teaching competence, modify their teaching behaviour and style, inculcate a scientific outlook, approach & attitude and help them transfer these to their learners.
6. ET supplements teacher in their instructional programmes through the structured lessons for remedial, enrichment or drill purposes.
7. The learners get the training of self-instruction and teachers are relieved of the burden of routine repetition for exercise & revision purposes

Objectives of educational technology

The objectives of educational technology are multifaceted and aim to improve the learning experience for everyone involved, from students to teachers to the education system as a whole.

Here are some key objectives:

Educational technology, with its vast tools and possibilities, has a range of objectives, both at the individual and broader societal levels. Let's delve into some key areas:

1)Enhancing Learning Outcomes:

- **Improve knowledge retention and understanding:** Interactive tools, simulations, and multimedia resources can make learning more engaging and effective, leading to better comprehension and long-term memory.
- **Personalize learning experiences:** Adaptive learning platforms, individualized feedback, and diverse resources can cater to different learning styles and paces, ensuring students learn at their best.
- **Develop critical thinking and problem-solving skills:** Interactive activities, virtual labs, and collaborative projects can encourage students to think critically, analyze information, and solve problems creatively.
- **Nurture communication and collaboration**: Online platforms and communication tools can foster teamwork, peer learning, and effective communication skills, crucial for the 21st century.

2)Promoting Engagement and Accessibility:

- **Make learning more interactive and enjoyable**: Gamification, simulations, and immersive experiences can transform learning into a fun and engaging process, boosting motivation and participation.
- **Increase access to education**: Online courses, digital resources, and mobile learning platforms can overcome geographical barriers and provide educational opportunities to underserved communities.
- **Support diverse learners**: Technology can provide tools and resources that cater to learners with different abilities and needs, fostering inclusive and equitable learning environments.

3)Developing 21st-Century Skills:

- **Equip students with digital literacy skills**: Technology tools can help students learn to navigate the digital world, critically evaluate information, and use technology responsibly and ethically.

- **Nurture creativity and innovation**: Digital tools like coding platforms, design software, and multimedia creation tools can empower students to explore their creativity and develop innovative solutions.
- **Prepare students for future careers**: Technology skills are increasingly valued in today's workforce, and EdTech can help students develop essential skills like data analysis, collaboration, and problem-solving in a technological context.

4)Beyond Individual Learning:

- **Improve instructional delivery**: Technology can provide teachers with tools for effective lesson planning, differentiated instruction, and real-time feedback, enhancing their teaching practices.
- **Streamline educational administration**: Online platforms can facilitate communication, manage data, and automate tasks, making school administration more efficient and effective.
- **Promote lifelong learning**: Online resources, MOOCs, and educational communities can provide opportunities for continuous learning and skill development throughout life. It's important to remember that these objectives are not mutually exclusive and often work together. The ultimate goal of educational technology is to empower learners, enhance learning experiences, and prepare them for a successful future in a technology-driven world.

1.2 Forms of educational technology- teaching technology, behavioral technology and instructional technology.

Introduction

- Teaching is the social and professional activity.
- Teaching is purposeful activity. The ultimate goal of teaching is to bring all round development of a child.
- Teaching is an art as well as science because teaching can be studied objectively and scientifically.
- The Chief exponents of Teaching Technology: I.K. Davies, N.L. Gagne, Herbert, Hunt, Burner and Robert Glaser.

- Teaching is such a classroom activity which is completed by the interaction between teachers and students.
- This activity leads to complete development of students.
- Today teaching is considered "Student-Centered" and not "Teacher Centered".
- In other words, instead of teaching by the teacher, the learning by the student is emphasized

Definitions

- For the new set up, education and training require a new conceptual framework against which decision involving change and innovation can be made" **Devies, 1971**
- "It is the application of philosophical, sociological and scientific knowledge to teaching for achieving some specific learning objectives" **R.A. Sharma, 1980**
- "Technology of teaching involves the know how the teaching process under specific conditions- it includes the mechanism of teaching process in the classroom situation, levels of teaching, principles operations and establishing relations between the learning tildes and teaching operations".- **A Scholar**

Content of Teaching Technology

I.K. Davies and Robert Glaser (1962) have developed the content of teaching technology and classified into 4 elements.

a. Planning of Teaching

b. Organization of teaching

c. Leading of teaching

d. Controlling of teaching

a) Planning of Teaching

A teacher makes proper plan to what he is to teach in the class. In planning he does 3 things/activities. i. Task analysis (He analyses the content and arranges such sub contents into systematic manner).

ii. Identification of Objectives (i.e. what changes he has to bring in the behaviourof his students).

iii. Writing learning Objectives (they can be evaluated at the end of the task).

B) Organization of Teaching

This stage is particularly related to the presentation of the subject matter. In organizing, a teacher does the following things,

i. He selects suitable teaching strategies and techniques.

ii. He selects or prepares suitable material aids for making the presentation of the subject-matter effective.

iii. He matches the strategies and material aids with the nature of the sub content to give such an experience to his students which is conducive to the realization of teaching objectives.

C) Leading of teaching

- This stage is related to communication strategies and reinforcement devices.
- The teacher motivates the students in such a way that learning becomes their necessity and they take full interest in the process.
- In order to learn various techniques of motivation, the teacher trainee is taught lessons like techniques of behaviour development, motivating devices, classroom behaviour model and observation of classroom behaviour.

D) Controlling of Teaching

- The last step concerns with evaluation of teaching.
- The main focus of this step is to assess the learning objectives in terms of student's performance.
- The learner's performance provides the basis for the feedback to teacher and learners.

Assumptions of Teaching Technology

The content of teaching technology is based on the following assumptions-

- Teaching is a scientific process and it has two major components: Content and Communication
- Teaching skills can be developed with the help of feedback devices.

- Teaching and learning are mutually inter-related means better teaching leads to better learning and better learning environment leads to better teaching.
- Modification and improvement can be made in teaching activities according to the situations (i.e.) there is no general formula applicable to all circumstances.
- Appropriate conditions can be created by teaching for effective learning.

Characteristics of Teaching Technology

- All the 3 domains of objectives: cognitive, affective and psychomotor can be achieved by this technology.
- Teaching technology is based on philosophical, sociological and scientific knowledge of education.
- Teaching can be organized at 3 levels namely: memory, understanding and reflective level of teaching.
- As a system it consists of the inputs, process and outputs with the focus on teachers.
- The teaching-learning process can be made effective with the help of teaching technology.

INSTRUCTIONAL TECHNOLOGY

INTRODUCTION

- The instruction has an important role in human learning. The systematic actions which induce learning is known as instruction.
- Instruction means communication of information by means other than a teacher. For example, various types of audio-visual aids can guide the students.
- The Correspondence Course and Open University students accomplish the task of instructions through press and television.
- Actually, instructional technology is based upon Hardware approach.
- It is based on psychological and scientific principles to instruction.

- The origin of IT is from psychological laboratory experiments.
- The most important example of IT is 'Programmed Instruction'.
- The Chief exponents of IT: B.F. Skinner, Robert Glaser, Norman A. Crowder, Mager, and Gilbert

Definition

- "Instructional technology means a network of techniques or devices employed to accomplish a set of learning objectives." R.A. Sharma 1980
- "The use of instructional technology is not only for software and hardware approach development but also for the implementation of underlying principles in these methods." – Mc Murin
- Robert E. Cox refers to this technology as a subordinate term of Teaching technology.

Content of Instructional Technology

- The instructional technology involves the strategies and tactics which can be used outside and inside the class room teaching.
- Teaching is an instruction but the instruction is not the teaching.

The instructional technology consists of the following content:

1. a. Meaning and definition of Instructional Technology,

   b. Definition of Programmed instruction and its Origin

   c. Meaning, assumptions, and Structure of Linear programming and its principles

   d. Meaning, assumptions, and Structure of Branching programming and its principles.

   e. Meaning, assumptions, principles, and instruction of mathematical programming.

   f. Learner-controlled instruction and computer-assisted instruction.

   g. Development of Programmed instruction material

      i. Planning, ii. Writing frames, iii. Evaluation.

      Teaching, Instruction and Programmed Instruction.

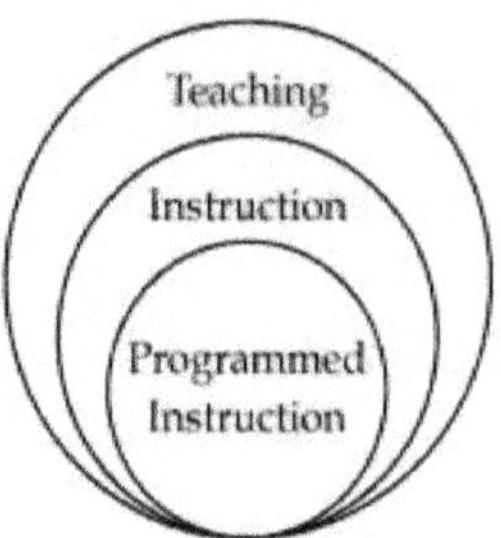

Assumptions of Instructional Technology

The instructional technology involves the following assumptions:

- A pupil can learn according to his needs and capacities.
- A pupil can learn even in the absence of the teacher.
- Reinforcement can be provided continuously by the use of instruction.
- The subject matter can be divided into its various elements and each element can be taught / presented independently through this technology.
- Students can be given feedback by instructional activities also, (i.e.) effective communication can provide feedback to learners.

Characteristics of Instructional Technology

- Objectives of Cognitive domain can be achieved by the use of this technology.
- Right responses of students can be reinforced regularly which will lead to further right responses to occur.
- By the use of this technology, students can learn according to their need and speed (rate).
- It provides the deep insight into the content structure and sequence of its elements.
- The instructional theory may be developed by using this technology in learning process.
- It helps in development of 'Learner-Centered' education.
- The instructional technology incorporates psychological learning theories and principles.
- The learning external conditions, contiguity practice, and reinforcement are created with the help of instruction.

- The instructional theory may be developed by using this technology in the learning process.
- The instructional technology can be employed in the storage of effective teachers.
- It provides a deep insight into the content structure and sequence of its elements

BEHAVIOURAL TECHNOLOGY: INTRODUCTION

- Behavior is a collective name of various activities of an individual.
- This technology is closely related to psychology.
- Psychology is the Science of behaviour and learning is the modification of behaviour through activities and experiences.
- It is an application of scientific knowledge or modifying teacher's behaviour.
- It is also called as 'Training Technology'.
- The chief exponents of B.T: Flanders, B.F. Skinner, Anderson, and Amidon.
- By N., Sam M.S. A range of experimentally-established techniques and approaches which are designed to effect behavioral change. It is a set of procedures accepted by scientists and influenced by scientific behavior analysis.
- "Behavioral technology is further supplemented by the latest research tools and clinical tests".

B.F. Skinnier has to referred term behavioral technologyin his book "Technology & Teaching"

Use of Technology to modify Behavior

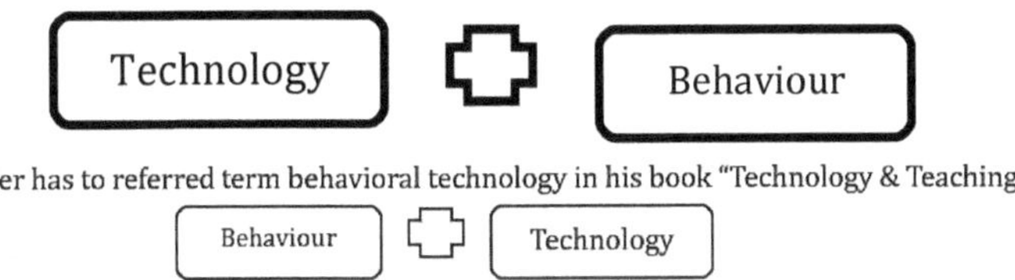

Use of Technology to modify Behavior

Content of Behavioural Technology

A teacher learns the following subject-matter (topics) under this technology:

- Meaning & definition of teaching & teacher behaviour .
- Methods of observing teacher's behaviour and its rating (speed).
- The interpretation and evaluation of teacher behaviour.
- Assumptions & theory of teacher behaviour.
- Models of classroom interaction.
- Various techniques of developing teacher behaviour such as,
  i. Micro teaching ii. Team teaching iii. Interaction analysis techniques
  iv. Simulated Social Skill Training.

Assumptions of Behavioral Technology

- The behaviour of the teacher is social as well as psychological.
- It means that psychological and social conditions directly affect teachers' behaviour.
- Teachers' behaviour can be observable
- Teachers' behaviour can be measurable.
- Teachers' behaviour is relative. It means that some teachers are good and some are not good.
- Teachers' behaviour can be modified by training and by using reinforcement devices.

Characteristics of Behavioural Technology

- It has the focus to achieve the psychomotor objectives.
- The specific teaching skills can be developed in teacher with the help of this technology.
- The basic foundation is psychology.
- It is based upon software approach.
- Reinforcement and feedback are emphasized.
- It aims at producing effective teachers by modifying their behaviour.
- It is more useful for teacher training institutions

Comparison among Different Forms of Educational Technology

Aspect Teaching	Teaching Technology	Instructional Technology	Behavioral Technology
1. Exponents	D. K Davies, N.L Gagne Herbert, Hunt, Bruner and Robert Glaser.	B. F Skinner, Glaser, Gilbert, Mager	Flanders, B.F Skinner, Anderson and Amidon
2, Objectives	Development of cognitive, affective and psychomotor domains.	Development of Cognitive domain.	Development of psychomotor (skills).
3. Components / approach	Content and communication	Physical (Hardware) approach	Behavioral (Software) approach
4. Basis / Foundation of teaching	Philosophical, sociological psychological and scientific	Psychological and scientific basis	Psychological and cybernetics.
5. content	- Planning of teaching - Organization of teaching - Leading of teaching - Controlling of teaching	- Task analysis - Formulating objectives in behavioral terms - Reinforcement strategies	- Teacher behaviour theories - Teaching models - Observation techniques - Analysis and modifications of Teacher behaviour.
6. Level / Types of teaching	- memory - understanding - Reflective	- Programmed learning (self)	- Interaction analysis - Micro Teaching - Team Teaching

and learning		- CAI - Learner Controlled Instruction	
7. Principles	- Art of teaching and science of learning	Input, Process, Output	Principles of learning feedback and reinforcement
8. Role of teacher	As Manage	As helper	As an observer or supervisor
9. Applicatio n	Improving classroom teaching and making it effective and purposive	Self – instruction, Corresponde nce education & remedial teaching	Teacher education and teacher training

1.3 Components of educational technology: hardware approach and software approach and systems approach- concept, process, steps and role of the teacher.

Educational technology consists of two interrelated concepts namely education and technology. Here, education refers to the process of overall development of child and technology involves highly designed and sophisticated engineering of software and hardware that is meant for the systematic organization of knowledge for practical purposes. In order to serve educational purposes, there is need of educational technology which helps in improving the processes as well as products of education. It is also called as learning technology which comprise of the use of technology in teaching-learning process. The basic idea behind the educational technology is "using all available resources (human and non-human) in a systematic manner to find viable solution to educational problems" (NCERT, 2006). With its first coinage, it referred to "technology in education", implying the use of a variety of educational audio-visual aids for teaching purposes. With further conceptual development of educational technology, the term "technology of education" came into vogue which looked at education in a wider sense, and included different aspects such as entry behavior of learners, objectives, contents, evaluation, etc. In addition, arrival of digital media added new dimension to educational technology (NCERT, 2006). The concept is not constant, but keeps on changing with changing time and scenario. Its scope and area is as wide as that of education itself.

"The universally accepted definition of educational technology involves processes, methods and techniques, products, resources and technologies, organized into workable system" (NCERT, 2006). In National Focus Group on Educational Technology, NCERT (2006), it is described as "the efficient organisation of any learning system adapting or adopting methods, processes, and products to serve identified educational goals. This involves systematic identification of the goals of education, recognition of the diversity of learner's needs, the contexts in which learning will take place, and the range of provisions needed for each of these."

Components of Educational Technology

In the field of education, educational technology has a wide range of scope and applicability. It helps in provision of necessary ways and means for brining improvement in the processes and products of teaching and learning. It makes practitioners search for new and innovatively effective ways of organizing teaching-learning processes. It has different aspects and forms such as teaching technology, instructional technology, behavioral technology and instructional design technology. Further, on the basis of the concepts of educational technology given in the introduction, it can be said that it is a "multi-faceted concept" (Mangal & Mangal, 2017). This multi-faceted concept has different components which can be understood in terms of the approaches to educational technology. According to ***Lumsdane*** Educational Technology can be classified to three distinct types on the basis of its multifaceted concept as follows.

1. Educational Technology I or Hardware Approach

2. Educational Technology II or Software Approach
3. Educational Technology III or System Approach

Hardware Approach

Hardware approach to educational technology is originated from physical sciences and engineering. This component is based on the concept of service which can be called as using technology in education. It adopts product-oriented approach where more concern is shown for production and utilization of audio-visual aid materials such as charts, models, slides, film strips, audio cassettes and sophisticated equipment such as radio, TV, films, projectors, tape recorders, video, teaching machine and computers (Mangal&Mangal, 2017). It strengthens the concept of utilizing these equipment and materials. It is also concerned with he advancement of mass media which contribute a lot to reach the educational benefits to masses with great ease and in more cost effective ways (Mangal&Mangal, 2017). This technology mechanizes the teaching-learning processes. According to Ruhela, "This part of educational technology refers to tools and hardware such as teaching machines, TV, tape recorder, etc. which are used in instructions. In fact, the selection and utilization of machines and hardware approaches in the field of learning is called hardware approach or educational technology I." Silverman called it 'relative technology' which refers to borrowing and to applying technology, machines and devices in the process of teaching and learning. By using these devices, teachers can deal with larger group of students to have discourse on teaching-learning experiences. Further, it is added that it utilizes the products of Software Technology for its functioning. It has the potential to hand over the educational benefits to the masses with greater ease and economy.

I- **Hardware Approach**

The hardware approach refers to the use of machines and other mechanical devices in the process of education. It originates from the physical sciences and engineering. The process of teaching-learning has been gradually mechanized through the use of teaching machines, radio, television, tape recorder, video-tape, projectors etc. The teacher can deal with a larger group of students at the same time by teaching through these machines. The hardware approach is based on the application of engineering principles for developing electro-mechanical equipment for instructional purposes. Motion pictures, tape recorders, television, teaching machines, computers are called educational hardware. Hardware approach mechanizes the process of teaching so that teachers would be able to deal with more students with less expenditures in educating them. Therefore, **the mechanization of teaching process is termed as Hardware Approach.**

Uses product-oriented techniques to shape of teaching learning material and strategy.

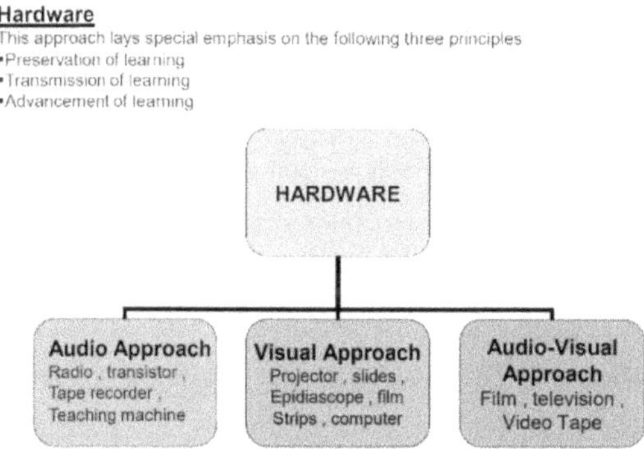

Characteristics of Hardware Approach

1. The concept of hardware approach is derived from the application of "physical science" to education.
2. Since technology is improving day by day, the use of Hardware Approach is making education change day by day. Therefore, Hardware Approach modernizes education.

3.Teachers need to have high level of computer literacy and willingness to adopt and make effective use of Hardware technology.
4.Engineering principles are used for the development of these types of technical equipment.
5.The teacher can deal with larger group of students with the help of machines.
6.It depends on Software Approach to be effective and successful.

II- Software Approach

Software approach originates from behavioural sciences and the application of psychology of learning. The biggest contributor to software approach was B.F Skinner. Software Approach is also termed as Instructional Technology or Teaching Technology.

Software approach refers to the application of teaching-learning principles from behavioral sciences to shape the behavior of students

. The software approach uses the principles of psychology formodifying his behaviour of students in a positive manner and developing vast amount of knowledge. Having originated from behavioural learning theories (Pavlov, Thorndike, Skinner etc.) the software approach tries to use

process-oriented techniques to develop suitable teaching learning tools, teaching materials, teaching strategies and evaluation methods. The product that is developed from this process is called a Software. Software Approach is concerned with teaching objectives in behavioral terms, principles of teaching, methods of teaching, reinforcement of instructional system, feedback, reviews and evaluation.

SOFTWARE APPROACH

In this approach emphasis is laid on developing all three aspects of education
Input
Output
Process

SOFTWARE APPROACH

GRAPHICS
Chart , graph , Map, posters , books

Demonstration
Chalk , flannel cardboard , bulletin Board , diagram and figures

Three–Dimensional
Models , Real objects

Characteristics of Software Approach

1.It is based on behavioural science and psychology of learning.

2.It uses the principles of psychology for the purpose of behaviour modification of students.

3.It develops all the three basic components of technology, i.e. Input, Process, Output.

4.Depends on Hardware Approach to be effective and successful.

2.4 Classification of Hardware and Software Approaches

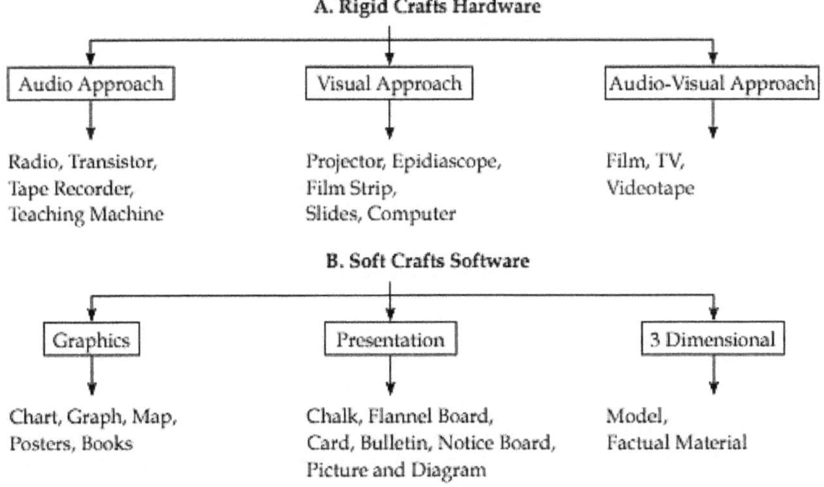

Hardware Approach	Software Approach
• It has its origin in physical sciences and applied engineering. • It is concerned with the production and utilization of audio-visual material, instruments and mass media for helping the teacher and learners in their tasks. • It adopts product-oriented approach. The products of software technology in the form of teaching learning materials and strategies are utilized by hardware instruments for effective teaching learning. • It is based on the concept of service. it stands for technology in education. • Hardware needs the services of software for its usage and functioning. • It has mass appeal and utilization. • It has resulted in improving the efficiency of educational means and reducing the costs of education. • Examples of hardware are radio, TV, tape recorder, video, slides and film projectors, computers, machines, etc.	• It has its origin in behavioural sciences and their applied aspects concerning psychology of learning. • It is concerned with the usage of psychology of learning for production and utilization of software techniques and materials for smoothening the teaching learning tasks. • It adopts process-oriented approach for production of materials. Produced materials are available to be used by the hardware appliances. • Software components do not provide direct services to its users. It stands for technology of education. • Productivity and usefulness of software approach is dependent on the case if it is assisted and made into use by hardware appliances and gadgets. • It does not have such appeal to masses. • It contributes in increasing the efficiency of teachers and learners.

	• Examples of software are programmed learning materials, strategies, etc.

III-Systems Approach / Educational Technology III

The third type of EdTech. Is **System Approach** or **System Analysis**. It is also known as **Management Technology**. It was developed after World War II. The origin of system approach is computer science. It aims to use computer science as a foundation for designing, applying and evaluating the educational system.

System Approach is an approach used to refer to the organization **as an organic and open system, which is composed of interacting and interdependent parts, called subsystems.**

- Systems approach is based on the idea that everything is inter-related and interdependent. A system is composed of related and dependent element which when in interaction, forms a unitary whole. A system is simply a combination of things or parts forming a complex whole. Just as a human body system is made up of various sub-systems (respiratory system, nervous systematic.)
- The Webster's dictionary defines a system as "a regularly interacting or interdependent group of items forming a unified whole". A system is "a group of objects related or interacting so as to farm a unity". It also defines the system as "organised or established procedure", or a "methodically arranged set of ideas, principles, methods or procedure". Systems analysis essentially is a systematic way of identifying goals of any system and scientifically working out the different steps to move towards these goals, suggesting "models" for application.
- The term "systems approach", "systems analysis" or "systems procedure" are used in literature at various levels of sophistication. At a layman's level, they indicate systematic thinking, step-by-step problem-solving and/or considering many variables not in isolation of each other but as interacting

with each other, studying the phenomenon as a whole and not in bits and pieces.

- Thus, the systems approach is an overall approach. It helps in designing a complex system by the efficient use of resources in the form of men, money, machines and materials so that the individual subsystem making up the total system can be designed and fitted together, checked operated so as to achieve the desired goal in the most efficient manner.
- According to Makridakis, "Systems approach is basically a way of thinking and it 'What is going on here' attitude which makes the systems way of thin and the major characteristics of the systems approach is its recognition the need to seek things".
- Systems approach is thus a rational, problem-solving method for analysing the educational process and making it more effective. System the process taken as a whole incorporating all its aspects and parts, pupils, teachers, curriculum content, instructional materials, instructional strategy, physical environment and the evaluation of instructional objectives. Hence it may be seen that the purpose of the systems analysis is the "best equipment in the best place for the best people at the best and at the best price".
- "The systems approach in instruction is an integrated, programme of complex instructional media, hardware and personnel whose components are structured as a single unit with a schedule of time and at sequential phasing".

The procedural steps in the system approach in education are as follows / Major Steps in Systems Approach

1. Formulating of specific instructional objectives to be achieved and defining instructional goals,
2. Deciding appropriate media to achieve these goals,
3. Defining learner characteristics and requirements,
4. Selecting appropriate methods suitable for effective learning to take place,
5. Selecting appropriate learning experiences from available alternatives,
6. Selecting appropriate materials and tools required,

7.Assigning appropriate personal roles for teachers, students and supporting staff,

8.Implementing the programme,

9.Evaluating the outcome in terms of original objectives measured in student performance and

10.Revising to improve efficiency of the system to improve students' learning.

ADVANTAGES OF SYSTEMS APPROACH

i. Systems approach helps to identify the suitability of the resource material to achieve the specific goal.

ii. Technological advance could be used to provide integration of machines, media and people for attaining the defined goal.

iii. It helps to assess the resource needs, their sources and facilities in relation to quantities, time and other factors.

iv. It permits an orderly introduction of components demonstrated to be required for systems success in terms of student learning.

v. It avoids rigidity in plan of action as continuous evaluation affords desired beneficial changes to be made.

LIMITATIONS OF SYSTEMS APPROACH

i. Resistance to change. Old ways are difficult to erase. There is always resistance to any new method or approach.

ii. Involves hard work. Systems approach requires hard and continuous work on the part of school personnel. Some are not prepared for the extra load.

iii. Lack of understanding. Teachers and administrators are still not familiar with systems approach. Though it has been successfully implemented industry, it has still to make headway in education.

ROLE OF THE TEACHER IN SYSTEM APPROACH

The general roles of the teacher in system approach are as follows:

a) Teacher has to formulate objectives

b) He has to assess to student entry behaviour and design and develop the system.
c) He should gong for improvement of the systems based on the analysis of resources of evaluation.
d) The role of the teacher consists building plans for implementing changes in the curriculum.
e) He has to choose the proper resource material for delivery of message.
f) It is prime duty to identify the resources and to develop resources if necessary. vii. He has to coordinate the curricular and co-curricular activities.
g) He has to integrate technological advances in the educational process

1.4 Importance of educational technology.

Educational technology, or EdTech for short, has become increasingly important in today's world, transforming how we learn and teach. Its significance stems from a variety of benefits it offers to both students and educators:

For Students:

- Enhanced Engagement and Motivation: EdTech tools can make learning more interactive and engaging, using multimedia content, simulations, and games to cater to diverse learning styles and keep students motivated.
- Personalized Learning: Technology allows for personalized learning paths, adapting to individual student needs and paces. Adaptive learning platforms recommend content based on a student's progress and mastery, while online courses offer flexible schedules and self-paced learning.
- Improved Access to Knowledge: EdTech democratizes education by providing access to a vast library of resources and learning materials beyond physical limitations. Online courses, educational apps, and digital libraries bridge geographical and socioeconomic barriers, making quality education more accessible to everyone.

- Development of Essential Skills: EdTech tools can help students develop crucial 21st-century skills, such as critical thinking, problem-solving, collaboration, and digital literacy. These skills are essential for success in the modern workforce and personal development.
- Increased Collaboration and Communication: EdTech platforms foster collaboration through online forums, virtual classrooms, and interactive tools, allowing students to learn from and with each other, regardless of location.

For Educators:

- Effective Teaching and Learning Strategies: EdTech tools provide educators with a variety of resources and strategies to enhance their teaching methods. Interactive whiteboards, presentation software, and assessment tools can make lessons more dynamic and effective, while data analytics can provide insights into student performance and inform teaching decisions.
- Improved Differentiation and Individualized Instruction: Technology allows educators to cater to the diverse needs of their students by providing personalized learning experiences and differentiated instruction. Online platforms and tools can help educators track student progress, identify learning gaps, and provide targeted support.
- Streamlined Administration and Communication: EdTech tools can streamline administrative tasks, such as grading, attendance tracking, and communication with parents, freeing up time for educators to focus on teaching and providing individual support to students.
- Professional Development and Growth: EdTech platforms offer educators access to online courses, professional development resources, and collaborative communities, enabling them to stay updated on the latest teaching methods and technologies.

Preparing students for the future:

- Developing essential skills: Educational technology can help students develop essential skills needed for success in the 21st century, such as digital literacy, critical thinking, problem-solving, and collaboration. These skills are increasingly important in today's workforce and can help students prepare for future careers.
- Promoting lifelong learning: Technology can foster a love of learning and encourage students to become lifelong learners. Access to online resources and educational platforms can provide students with opportunities to continue learning and exploring new interests throughout their lives.

However, it's important to remember that EdTech is a tool, not a silver bullet. Its effectiveness depends on its appropriate integration into the learning process, with a focus on pedagogy and student-centered learning.

Overall, EdTech plays a crucial role in transforming education by making it more engaging, personalized, accessible, and effective for both students and educators. As technology continues to evolve, its impact on education is likely to become even more profound, shaping the future of learning and preparing students for success in the 21st century.

UNIT 2: FUNDAMENTALS OF COMPUTER

2.1 Meaning and Characteristics of Computer.

A computer is an electronic device that can store, manipulate, and process data according to a set of instructions. Know more about the Computer and its Classification, Characteristics, Functionality.

What is a computer?

In the modern world, computers have become an integral part of our daily lives, revolutionizing the way we work, communicate, and entertain ourselves. From desktops to laptops, tablets to smartphones, computers come in various forms, yet many people are still unfamiliar with their inner workings and potential. In this article, we will discuss everything about the Computer Definition, Characteristics, Components, Functionality, and Classification.

Definition of Computer

A computer is an electronic device wherein we need to input raw data to be processed with a set of programs to produce a desirable output. Computers have the ability to store, process, and manipulate data. The term "computer" is derived from the Latin word "Computer," which means "to calculate." A computer is made to run programs and apps by using both hardware and software. It also has a memory to store data, programs, and what they produce.

Characteristics of Computer

Computers are now an integral part of our daily lives, from managing student records in schools to handling patient records in hospitals. They have significantly simplified our tasks. Now, we can quickly access stored data and solve complex problems in just seconds.

Characteristics of Computers:

- **Saves Time**: A computer saves time by completing tasks quicker and more efficiently. For example, it can solve big complex problems within seconds which can save many minutes of ours.

- **Internet**: Computers connect us to the internet which can help us to know important information from around the world, it can connect us with people from around the world through social networking sites, etc.
- **Storage:** The computer gives us enough storage space that can be used to store a large amount of data including your projects, eBooks, documents, movies, pictures, songs, etc.
- **Entertainment**: Computers are also a big source of entertainment as you can play games, listen to songs, watch movies, and can also use social networking sites.
- **Organized Data:** It not only stores the data for you for also organizes the data for you. You can create different folders for different types of data and can easily access them when required.
- **Helps the physically challenged:** Computers are a big boon for the physically challenged people as Stephen Hawking, who was not able to speak used the computer to speak. It also can be used to help blind people by installing special software to read what is on the screen.
- **Features OF Computer**
- We have discussed a few points that will highlight the different features of computers. These features collectively contribute to the versatility and functionality of computers.
- **Processing Power:** Computers can execute instructions and perform calculations quickly.
- Storage Capacity: They can store vast amounts of data, from documents to multimedia files.
- **Memory (RAM):** Temporary storage used for actively running programs and processes.
- Input Devices: Keyboards, mouse, and other peripherals allow users to input data.
- Output Data: Monitors, printers, and speakers display or produce results.

- **Upgradability**: Components like RAM, storage, and graphics cards can be upgraded.
- **Portability:** Laptops and tablets offer mobility compared to desktop computers.
- **User Interface**: Graphical user interfaces (GUIs) or command-line interfaces for interaction.
- **Security Features**: Passwords, firewalls, and antivirus tools protect against unauthorized access.

Power Management: Features to optimize energy consumption.

History of Computer

To understand the development of computers, and how they evolved from simple mechanical devices to the complex electronic machines that we use today. The knowledge can help to appreciate the challenges that computer scientists have faced over the years and the ingenuity they have shown in overcoming them.

Studying the history of computers can help to anticipate future developments in the field. The history of computers can be traced back to the ancient Greeks, who used the abacus to perform simple calculations. In the 17th century, Blaise Pascal invented the mechanical calculator, which could perform more complex calculations. In the 19th century, Charles Babbage designed the Analytical Engine, which is considered to be the first general-purpose computer. By understanding the history of computers that have shaped the development in the past.

Classification of Computers

Computers come in various types, primarily categorized by their data handling capacity and physical size. Based on the size, computers are 5 types namely, Micro Computer, Mini Computer, Mainframe Computer, Super Computer and Work stations. Whereas, based on data handling capacity, there are 3 types of computers namely analogue computers, digital computers, and hybrid computers. All the different types of computers perform different tasks and have been designed differently. For your reference, we have discussed all the types of computers and you can scroll through the page to read them all.

Based on Size

There are various types of computers available in the markets which are of different sizes. These computers are different from each other with respect to the amount of work they can do or the amount of data they can hold. Here we have classified the main 5 types of computers based on their size and have also provided the details regarding the same.

Types of Computers	Description
Micro Computers	Microcomputers are small, affordable computers for personal use. Examples include desktops and laptops. They handle everyday tasks like browsing, word processing, and entertainment.
Mini-computers	Minicomputers are mid-sized computers, more powerful than personal computers but smaller than mainframes. They handle complex tasks for businesses and institutions, offering moderate processing capabilities.
Mainframe Computers	Mainframe computers are powerful computers used by large organizations for critical applications and data processing
Super Computer	Supercomputers are high-performance machines used for complex calculations, simulations, and scientific research.
Work stations	Workstations are advanced computers used for graphics, engineering, and scientific applications

1. Micro Computer:

Micro Computers are mainly single-user computers and have comparatively lesser storage and speed than other computers. The first microcomputer was built with 8-bit microprocessor chips as these computers use microprocessors as CPU. Laptops, smartphones, desktop computers, etc. are all examples of microcomputers. These computers are made for everyday tasks like browsing the web and using programs like Microsoft Office MS Word etc.

2. Mini Computer:

Midrange computers or Mini-computers are multi-user computers designed in a way so as to entertain multiple users simultaneously. Small businesses and firms use these computers for their specific purposes. For example- a company or organization may use mini computers to look after the employee directory which may handle the payment history of its employees and any schools may use them to keep records of the students or for admission purposes.

3. Mainframe Computer:

Mainframe Computers are also not designed for single users, rather it is a multi-user computer that can handle thousands of users all at once. Large industries and government organizations utilize these computers to facilitate their business operations by storing substantial volumes of data. Banks and insurance companies use these computers to store the data of their customers, their policies, etc.

4. Super Computer:

Super Computer is the fastest type of computer amongst all and is also the most expensive. They can store a large number of data and can perform the most complex tasks within seconds. They can also execute millions of instructions per second. These computers are designed specifically to handle specific tasks such as weather forecasting, space research, and more. Supercomputers are also used by NASA for their Satellite launching.

5. Work Stations:

Workstations are single-user computers and have more powerful microprocessors than a microcomputer. When it comes to speed and storage capacity, it comes between a personal computer and a mini-computer. The most common uses of a workstation are desktop publishing, engineering designs, etc.

Functionality of a Computer

Computers possess remarkable versatility and can perform a multitude of tasks. Some basic functionalities and uses of a computer are shown below.

Data Processing: Computers excel at processing vast amounts of data quickly and accurately. They can manipulate numbers, perform complex calculations, analyze patterns, and generate reports.

Information Storage: With their vast storage capacities, computers can store massive amounts of information, from personal files to entire databases. They enable quick retrieval and organization of data for efficient access and analysis.

Communication: Computers facilitate seamless communication through various means, such as email, instant messaging, video conferencing, and social media. They enable global connectivity and information sharing on an unprecedented scale.

Multimedia and Entertainment: Computers serve as multimedia powerhouses, allowing users to watch movies, listen to music, view images, play games, and edit videos. They provide immersive experiences and entertainment options for users of all ages

Finally, a computer is a remarkable electronic device that processes data, performs calculations, and executes tasks based on programmed instructions. It comprises various components working together to facilitate the input, processing, and output of information. From their ability to process data at incredible speeds to their role in communication, entertainment, and information storage, computers have revolutionized every aspect of our lives. The computer was invented by Charles Babbage. So, he is known as the father of computers.

2.2 Computer Hardware: Input Devices (Text, audio, image, video). Output Devices (Text, audio, image, video). Memory Devices (Primary and Secondary).

Computer Hardware: Input Devices (Text, audio, image, video)

The computer system is designed to perform tasks given by the user and produce results efficiently. It takes in the instructions (in the form of inputs), performs the computing tasks (also known as processing) and gives back results (in the form of outputs). The computer's software is designed to do this task with the help of components of a computer, including an input unit, a processing unit, and an output unit. The computer performs the tasks with the combination of input and output devices to give instructions to the computer and receive the respective results of the operations performed.

Input Devices

An input device is a hardware device that takes instructions from the user and passes it to a processing unit, such as a CPU. Input devices can transmit data to other devices by taking it from one device but cannot receive data—for example, the keyboard or the mouse.

• Any peripheral (piece of computer hardware equipment) used to provide data and control signals to a computer.

• Allows the user to put data into the computer.

• Without any input devices, a computer would only be a display device and not allow users to interact with it.

Examples of Input Device

• Keyboard • Mouse • Touchscreen • Graphic tablet • Microphone • Scanner

Keyboard

• One of the primary input devices used with a computer.

• The keyboard looks very similar to the keyboards of electric typewriters, with some additional keys.

• Keyboards allow a computer user to input letters, numbers, and other symbols into a computer

• Uses an arrangement of buttons or keys.

• Requires pressing and holding several keys simultaneously or in sequence.

Types of Keyboard Standard

• Desktop computer keyboards, such as the 101-key US traditional keyboards or the 104-key Windows keyboards, include alphabetic characters, punctuation symbols, numbers and a variety of function keys.

Laptop Keyboard

• The laptop computer keyboard is a small version of the typical QWERTY keyboard.

• A typical laptop has the same keyboard type as a normal keyboard, except for the fact that most laptop keyboards condense the symbols into fewer buttons to accommodate less space.

Gaming and Multimedia Keyboard • The gaming keyboards are designed for the convenience of the gamers and these types of keyboards provide the required controls on the keyboards like back lighting.

Thumb -sized keyboard • Smaller external keyboards have been introduced for devices without a built -in keyboard, such as PDAs, and smartphones. • Small keyboards are also useful where there is a limited workspace.

Virtual Keyboard • The virtual keyboards are not actually physical keyboards, but they are simulated using a software.

Foldable Keyboard • Foldable keyboards are extremely good for travelling. • Simply roll them up and then unroll them when you need them again.

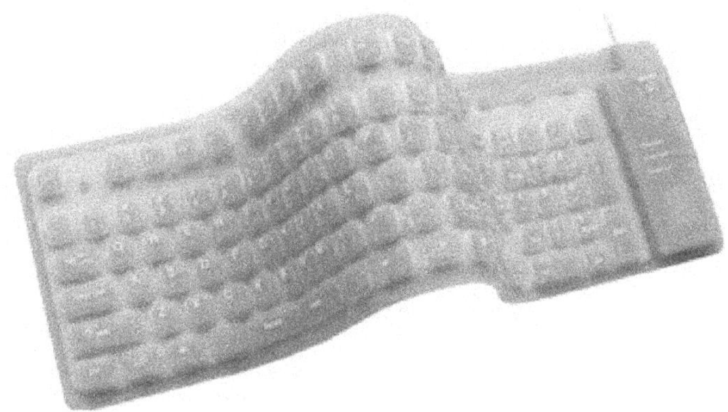

Keyboard Layouts • QWERTY • QWERTZ • AZERTY • DVORAK

QWERTY • Common layout

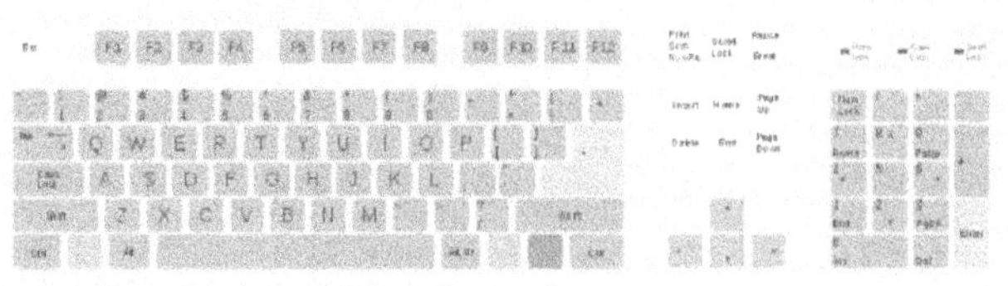

QWERTZ • Used in Germany, Hungary and Czech Republic

AZERTY • It is used by most French speakers based in Europe

DVORAK • Alternative for QWERTY • Dvorak layout uses less finger motion, increases typing rate, and reduces errors compared to the standard QWERTY

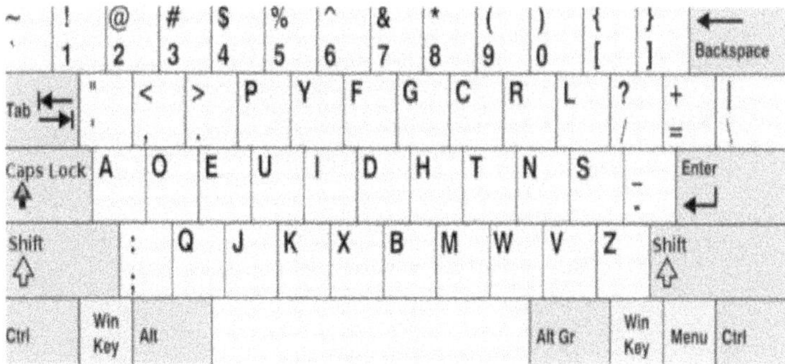

Key Types

Key Type	Example
Alphanumeric	A-Z, 0-9
Punctuation	. , ! " ?
Modifiers	Shift, Space Bar, Enter, Ctrl, Alt
Navigation	Arrows, Home, Page Up
System Command	PrtScn, Esc, F1, Start

Function keys

• The Function keys or F1 through F12 keys are used in programs as shortcut keys to performed frequently performed tasks. • For example, the F1 key is the key to open the online help for most programs.

Control Keys

• The Control keys are what give you additional control of a document. Keypad

• Although not available on all computer keyboards, especially laptops; the keypad gives the user a quick access to numbers and math functions such as plus, divide, times, and subtract.

Arrow keys

• The arrow keys are four directional arrow keys that allow the user to move their cursor and position on a page.

Keyboard Shortcut Keys

Shortcut Keys	Description
Alt + F	File menu options in current program.
Alt + E	Edit options in current program
F1	Universal Help in almost every Windows program.
Ctrl + A	Select all text.
Ctrl + X	Cut selected item.
Shift + Del	Cut selected item.
Ctrl + C	Copy selected item.
Ctrl + Ins	Copy selected item
Ctrl + V	Paste
Shift + Ins	Paste
Ctrl + P	Print the current page or document.
Home	Goes to beginning of current line.
Ctrl + Home	Goes to beginning of document.
End	Goes to end of current line.
Ctrl + End	Goes to end of document.
Shift + Home	Highlights from current position to beginning of line.
Shift + End	Highlights from current position to end of line.
Ctrl + Left arrow	Moves one word to the left at a time.
Ctrl + Right arrow	Moves one word to the right at a time.

II-Pointing Devices

• A pointing device is a hardware input device that allows the user to move the mouse pointer to select items on a display screen. • Types of pointing device: – Based on rolling a ball – Based on touching a surface – Based on moving stick

Based on rolling a ball

• Example: – Mouse – Trackball

Mouse

• A device that controls the movement of the cursor or pointer on a display screen.

• The mouse is important for graphical user interfaces because user can simply point to options and objects and click a mouse button.

Type of Mouse • Mechanical: Has a rubber or metal ball on its underside that can roll in all directions. • Optical: Uses a laser to detect the mouse's movement.

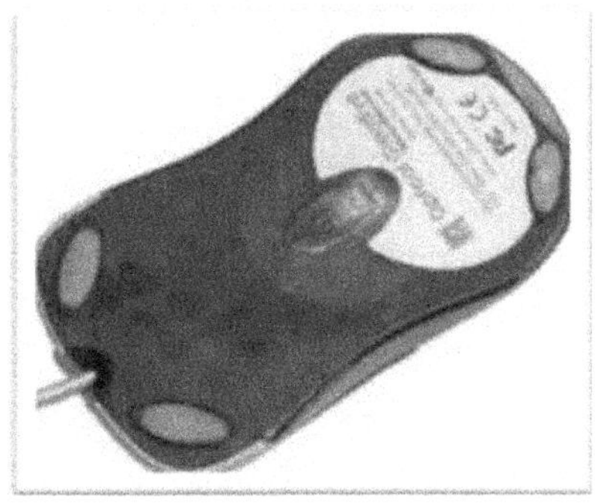

Trackball

• A trackball is a mouse lying on its back.

• To move the pointer, you rotate the ball with your thumb, your fingers, or the palm of your hand. • It does not require much space to use it

Based on touching a surface

• Example: – Touchpad – Graphic tablet – Touch screen – Light pen – Stylus

Touchpad • A small, touch-sensitive pad used as a pointing device on some portable computers. • By moving a finger or other object along the pad, you can move the pointer on the display screen.

Graphic Tablet • A graphics tablet (or digitizer, digitizing tablet, graphics pad, drawing tablet) is a computer input device that allows one to hand draw images and graphics, similar to the way one draws images with a pencil and paper.

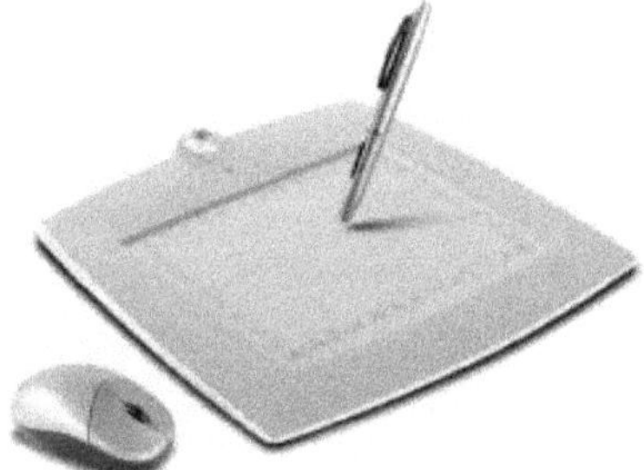

Touchscreen • A touchscreen is an electronic visual display that can detect the presence and location of a touch within the display area. • The term generally refers to touching the display of the device with a finger or hand.

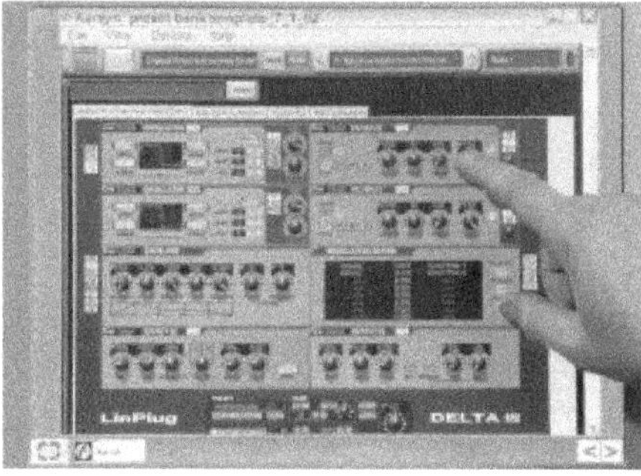

Light Pen • A light pen is a computer input device in the form of a light sensitive wand used in conjunction with a computer's CRT display. • It allows the user to point to displayed objects or draw on the screen in a similar way to a touchscreen but with greater positional accuracy.

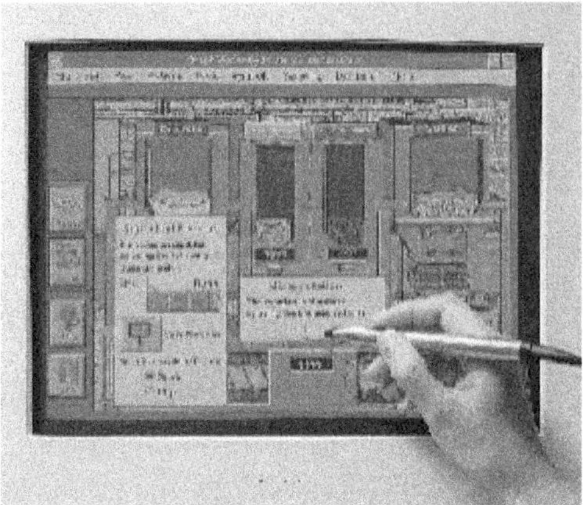

Stylus • A stylus is a small pen-shaped instrument that is used to input commands to a computer screen, mobile device or graphics tablet.

Based on moving stick • Example: – Joystick – Gamepad
Joystick • A joystick allows an individual to move an object in a game such as navigating a plane in a flight simulator.

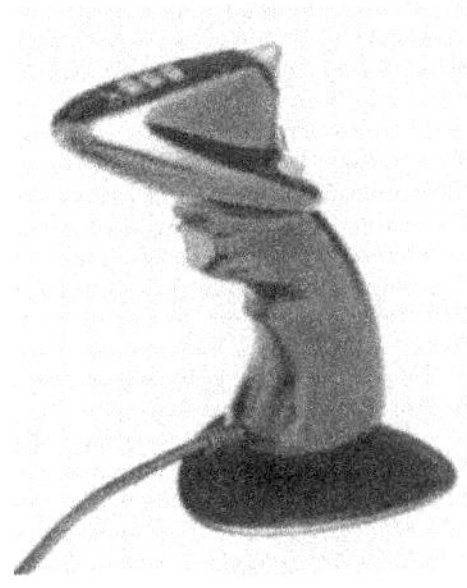

Gamepad • A gamepad, game controller, joypad, or video game controller is a peripheral device designed to be connected to a computer or console gaming system. • It has multiple buttons and may have one or two mini joysticks.

Imaging and Video Input Devices

• Used to digitize images or video from the outside world into the computer.

• Example: – Digital camera – Webcam – Optical scanner – 3D scanner – Fingerprint scanner – Barcode reader

Digital Camera

• A camera that stores the pictures or video it takes in electronic format instead of to film. • Digital cameras have become the camera solution for most users today as the quality of the picture they take has greatly improved and as the price has decreased.

Webcam

• A webcam is a hardware camera connected to a computer that allows anyone connected to the Internet to view either still pictures or motion video of a user or other object.

Optical Scanner • An optical scanner is a hardware input device that allows a user to take an image or text and convert it into a digital file, allowing the computer to read or display the scanned object. • **Two types of scanners: – Flatbed – Hand-held**

Image Scanner

Flatbed Scanner

Hand-held Scanner

Flatbed Scanner	Handheld Scanner
Flatbed scanners look similar to a small photocopier with the document remaining flat and stationary during the scanning	Hand-held scanners are used for entering text and images that are less than a page wide. Hand-held scanners are adequate for small pictures and photos but are difficult for entire pages.

3D Scanner • A 3D scanner is a device that analyzes a real-world object or environment to collect data on its shape and possibly its appearance (i.e. color). • The collected data can then be used to construct digital, three dimensional models.

Fingerprint Scanner • A fingerprint scanner or fingerprint reader is a hardware device that verifies a user or enters password information by scanning their finger.

Barcode Reader • A barcode reader or scanner is a hardware device capable of reading a barcode and printing out the details of the product or logging that product into a database.

Audio Input Devices

• Audio input devices allow a user to send audio signals to a computer for processing, recording, or carrying out commands. • Example: – Microphone – MIDI keyboard

Microphone • A microphone is a hardware peripheral that allows computer users to input audio into their computers.

MIDI Keyboard • A MIDI (Musical Instruments Digital Interface) keyboard is typically a piano-style user interface keyboard device used for sending MIDI signals to a computer. • MIDI information is sent to a computer that capable of reproducing an array of digital sounds or samples that resemble traditional analog musical instruments.

Output Devices (Text, audio, image, video)

The output device displays the result of the processing of raw data that is entered in the computer through an input device. There are a number of output devices that display output in different ways such as text, images, hard copies, and audio or video. They bridge the gap between digital data and human perception, letting users engage with computer-generated information. Understanding the many forms of output devices and their importance in computing is essential for making informed decisions while selecting the right devices for certain applications.

Categories of Output Devices

Output devices can be categorized into four main types based on the nature of their output.

- **Visual Output Devices:** These devices display processed data as text, images, or video. Examples include monitors and projectors, which allow users to view information on screens or project it onto larger surfaces.
- **Data Output Devices:** These devices provide machine-readable output for further processing or storage. Plotters and 3D printers fall into this category, allowing users to create physical representations of data or objects.
- **Print Output Devices:** Printers produce hard copies of processed data, such as documents, images, or graphics. They allow for physical documentation and distribution of information.
- **Sound Output Devices:** These devices deliver audio output for listening or communication purposes. Speakers and headphones/earphones enable users to hear the sound, whether Music, speech, or other audio content.

Output Devices • Any peripheral that receives or displays output from a computer. • Computer hardware equipment used to communicate the results of data processing carried out by a computer to the outside world.

Examples of Output Device • Monitor • Printer • Speakers • Projector

Monitor • The device which displays computer output. • The monitor displays the video and graphics information generated by the computer through the video card. • Monitors are very similar to televisions but usually display information at a much higher resolution.

Monochrome Monitor

• A monochrome monitor is a type of CRT computer display which was very common in the early days of computing, from the 1960s through the 1980s, before color monitors became popular.

• They are still widely used in applications such as computerized cash register systems.
• Monochrome monitors actually display two colors, one for the background and one for the foreground. • The colors can be black and white, green and black, or amber and black.

Color Monitor
• Color monitors can display anywhere from 16 to over 1 million different colors. • Color monitors are sometimes called RGB monitors because they accept three separate signals -- red, green, and blue.

Types of Monitors • Cathode Ray Tube (CRT) • Liquid Crystal Display (LCD) • Light-emitting Diode (LED)
Cathode Ray Tube (CRT) • Large • Heavy • Produce heat • Not expensive

Liquid Crystal Display (LCD) • Less space • Lighter • Low power consumption • Expensive • Limited viewing angle.

Light-emitting Diode (LED) • Less space • Lighter • Very expensive • Provide higher contrast and better viewing angles than LCD monitor.

Screen Size • The actual amount of screen space that is available to display a picture, video or working space • Desktop screens are usually 14 - 25 inches by diagonal measurement.

Aspect Ratio • The aspect ratio of a display is the fractional relation of the width of the display area compared to its height. • Two common aspect ratios: – 4:3 – 16:9

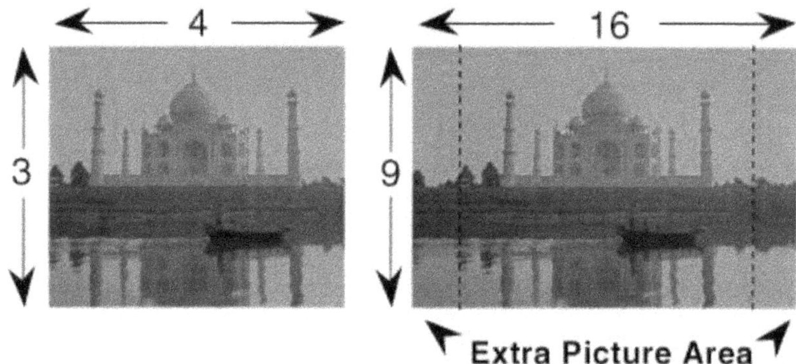

Display Resolution • The resolution of a monitor indicates how densely packed the pixels are. • In general, the more pixels (often expressed in dots per inch), the sharper the image. • Most modern monitors can display 1024 by 768 pixels, the SVGA standard. • Some high-end models can display 1280 by 1024, or even 1600 by 1200.

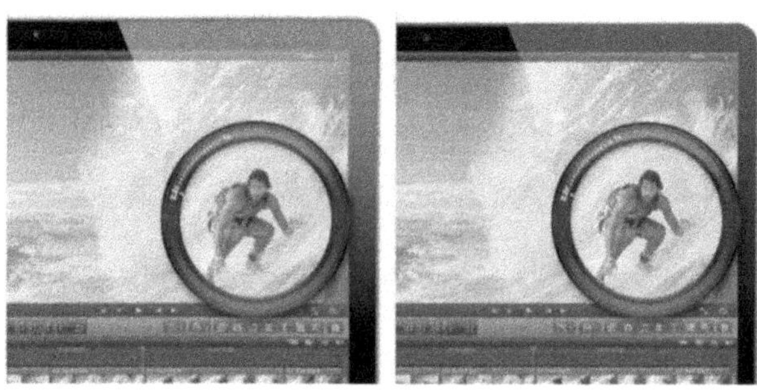

Monitor Features Refresh Rate • The refresh rate is the number of times in a second that a monitor draws the data. • The refresh rate for a monitor is measured in hertz (Hz) • The standard refresh rate is 75Hz, this means that the monitor redraws the display 75 times per second. • A flickering monitor can contribute to eyestrain and headaches. • The faster the refresh rate, the less the monitor flickers.

Monitor flickering

Color Depth • Color depth describes how many colors that can be displayed on a monitor's screen. • Common color depths used by monitor: – 4-bit (EGA) = 16 colors – 8-bit (VGA) = 256 colors – 16-bit (High Color) = 65,536 colors – 24-bit (True Color) = 16 million colors.

EGA Monitor VGA Monitor

Printer

• Printer is an external hardware device responsible for taking computer data and generating a hard copy of that data.

• Printers are one of the most used peripherals on computers and are commonly used to print text, images, and photos.

Types of Printer Printers can be categorized into: • Impact Printer • Non-Impact Printer

Impact Printer • It strikes paper and ribbon together to form a character, like a typewriter.

Advantages	Disadvantages
• Less expensive • Can make multiple copies with multipart paper	• Noisy • Print quality lower in some types • Poor graphics or none at all • Slow

Impact Printer

Daisy-wheel • Similar to a ball-head typewriter, this type of printer has a plastic or metal wheel on which the shape of each character stands out in relief. • A hammer presses the wheel against a ribbon, which in turn makes an ink stain in the shape of the character on the paper. • Daisy-wheel printers produce letter-quality print but cannot print graphics.

Dot-Matrix • Creates characters by striking pins against an ink ribbon. • Each pin makes a dot, and combinations of dots form characters and illustrations.

Non-Impact Printer • It uses ink spray, toner powder or inkless

Advantages	Disadvantages
• Quiet • Can handle graphics and often a wider variety of fonts than impact printers • Fast	• More expensive • Occupies a lot of space • The cost of maintaining it is high

Laser Printer (Toner-based)

• A laser printer rapidly produces high quality text and graphics.

• Laser printers are often used in corporate, school, and other environments that require print jobs to be completed quickly and in large quantities.

Multifunction Printer (Toner-based) • An MFP is an office machine which incorporates the functionality of multiple devices in one. • A typical MFP may act as a combination of some or all of the following devices: – Printer – Scanner – Photocopier – Fax CSCA0101 Computing Basi

Ink-jet Printer

• Inkjet printer operates by propelling variably-sized droplets of liquid or molten material (ink) onto almost any sized page. • They are the most common type of computer printer used by consumers.

Thermal Printer (Inkless) • Thermal printers work by selectively heating regions of special heat sensitive paper. • These printers are commonly used in calculators and fax machines; and although they are inexpensive and print relatively fast, they produce low resolution print jobs.

Printing Speed The printing speed is measured in: • cps (characters per second) • lpm (lines per minute) • ppm (pages per minute)

Plotter • The plotter is a computer printer for printing vector graphics • Plotters are used in applications such as computer aided design such as diagrams, layouts, specification sheets and banners • The plotter is capable of producing color drawings in a matter of minutes • Plotters differ from printers in that they draw lines using a pen • Plotters are considerably more expensive than printers.

Speakers

• A hardware device connected to a computer's sound card that outputs sounds generated by the computer. • Speakers can be used for various sounds meant to alert the user, as well as music and spoken text.

Headphones • Headphones give sound output from the computer. • They are similar to speakers, except they are worn on the ears so only one person can hear the output at a time.

Projector • An output device that can take the display of a computer screen and project a large version of it onto a flat surface. • Projectors are often used in meetings and presentations so that everyone in the room can view the presentation.

Types of projectors • Cathode Ray Tube (CRT) projector • Liquid Crystal Display (LCD) projector • Digital Light Processing (DLP) projector.

Cathode Ray Tube (CRT) projector • In the early days of projectors, CRT projectors were commonly used. • They utilized three tubes, one for each of the primary colors. • Due to their large size, low light output and the frequent need to converge and align the images projected from each of the three tubes, they are no longer commonly used. •Long service life; CRT tubes maintain good brightness to 10,000 hours. • CRT projectors are both considerably larger and heavier than comparable LCD and DLP projectors. • CRT projectors require far more time to set up and adjust than LCD and DLP based projectors.

Liquid Crystal Display (LCD) projector

• LCD projectors work by utilizing polarized mirrors that pass and reflect only certain colors of light.

• This causes each channel of red, green and blue to be separated and later re-converged via a prism after passing through an LCD panel that controls the intensity and saturation of each color.

•An LCD projector can achieve greater brightness at a lower energy consumption

• Smaller than CRT projectors

Digital Light Processing (DLP) projector • DLP projectors can be classified as one-chip or three-chip. • One-chip DLP projectors can produce more than 16 million colors while three-chip models can produce more than 35 trillion colors. • This allows DLP projectors to reproduce more natural and lifelike images.

III-Memory Devices (Primary and Secondary)

What is computer memory?

Computer memory is a data storage technology that is capable of storing or saving data, temporarily or permanently. The data stored are in a binary form such as 0 and 1 as well, allowing the user to save and retrieve the information anytime they require it.

Why is computer memory so important?

You can imagine computer memory to be a human brain, a computer memory provides the computer space to access data quickly. This would then allow the processor to communicate with the program much quicker. Without computer memory, the user wouldn't be able to save anything as well, which makes it incredibly important!

1.Computer Data Storage 2. Types of Storage 3. Storage Device Features 4. Other Examples of Storage Device

A storage device is used in the computers to store the data. • Provides one of the core functions of the modern computer.

There are four types of storage: • Primary Storage • Secondary Storage • Tertiary Storage • Off-line Storage

Primary Storage • Also known as main memory. • Main memory is directly or indirectly connected to the central processing unit via a memory bus. • The CPU continuously reads instructions stored there and executes them as required. • Example: – RAM – ROM – Cache

RAM • It is called Random Access Memory because any of the data in RAM can be accessed just as fast as any of the other data. •

There are two types of RAM: – DRAM (Dynamic Random Access Memory) – SRAM (Static Random Access Memory)

Static RAM	Dynamic RAM
• Faster • More expensive • More power consumption • does not need to be refreshed	• Slower • Less expensive • Less power consumption • needs to be refreshed thousands of times per second

ROM • This memory is used as the computer begins to boot up (Read only Memory) • Small programs called firmware are often stored in ROM chips on hardware devices (like a BIOS chip), and they contain instructions the computer can use in performing some of the most basic operations required to operate hardware devices. • ROM memory cannot be easily or quickly overwritten or modified.

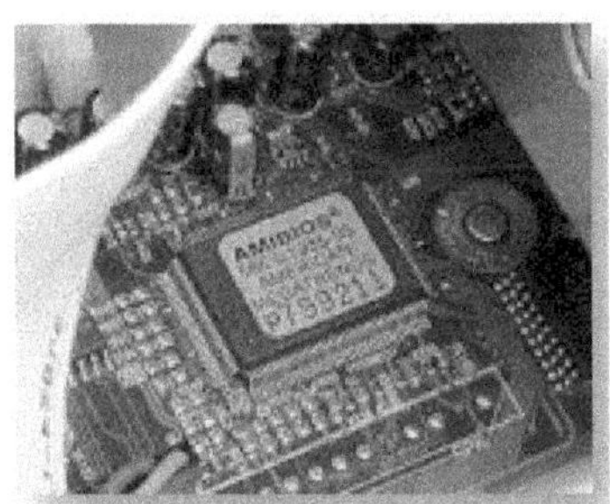

Cache • Cache is a high-speed access area that can be either a reserved section of main memory or a storage device. • Most computers today come with L3 cache or L2 cache, while older computers included only L1 cache.

Secondary Storage • It is not directly accessible by the CPU. • Computer usually uses its input/output channels to access secondary storage and transfers the desired data using intermediate area in primary storage. • Example: – Hard disk

Hard Disk • The hard disk drive is the main, and usually largest, data storage device in a computer. • It can store anywhere from 160 gigabytes to 2 terabytes. • Hard disk speed is the speed at which content can be read and written on a hard disk. • A hard disk unit comes with a set rotation speed varying from 4500 to 7200 rpm. • Disk access time is measured in milliseconds.

Internal Hard disk External Hard disk

	Internal Hard disk	External Hard disk
Portability	No	Yes
Price	Less expensive	More expensive
Speed	Fast	Slow
Size	Big	Small

Tertiary Storage

• Typically, it involves a robotic mechanism which will mount (insert) and dismount removable mass storage media into a storage device.

• It is a comprehensive computer storage system that is usually very slow, so it is usually used to archive data that is not accessed frequently.

• This is primarily useful for extraordinarily large data stores, accessed without human operators.

Examples: – Magnetic Tape – Optical Disc

Magnetic Tape

• A magnetically coated strip of plastic on which data can be encoded.

• Tapes for computers are similar to tapes used to store music.

• Tape is much less expensive than other storage mediums but commonly a much slower solution that is commonly used for backup.

Optical Disc • Optical disc is any storage media that holds content in digital format and is read using a laser assembly is considered optical media. • The most common types of optical media are – Blu-ray (BD) – Compact Disc (CD) – Digital Versatile Disc (DVD)

	CD	DVD	BD
Capacity	700MB	4.7GB – 17GB	50GB
Wavelength	780nm	650nm	405nm
Read/Write Speed	1200KB/s	10.5MB/s	36MB/s
Example	• CD-ROM, • CD-R • CD-RW	• DVD-ROM • DVD+R/RW • DVD-R/RW • DVD-RAM	• BD-R • BD-RE

Off-line Storage • Also known as disconnected storage. • Is a computer data storage on a medium or a device that is not under the control of a processing unit. • It must be inserted or connected by a human operator before a computer can access it again.
Examples: – Floppy Disk – Zip diskette – USB Flash drive – Memory card.
Floppy Disk • A soft magnetic disk. • Floppy disks are portable. • Floppy disks are slower to access than hard disks and have less storage capacity, but they are much less expensive. • Can store data up to 1.44MB. • Two common sizes: 5 ¼" and 3 ½".

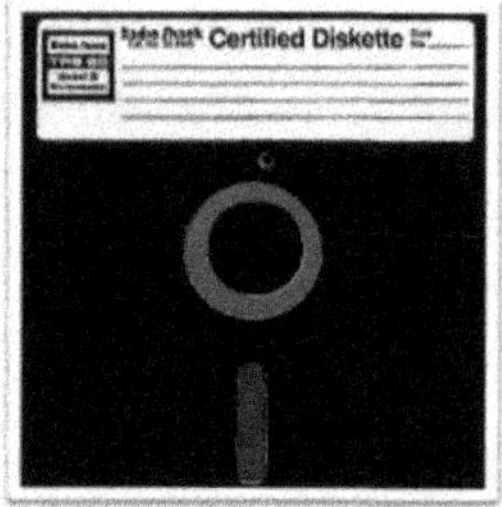

5 ¼ inch Floppy Disk 3 ½ inch Floppy Disk

Zip Diskette • Hardware data storage device developed by Iomega that functions like a Standard 1.44" floppy drive. • Capable to hold up to 100 MB of data or 250 MB of data on new drives. • Now it less popular as users needed larger storage capabilities.

USB Flash Drive • A small, portable flash memory card that plugs into a computer's USB port and functions as a portable hard drive. • Flash drives are available in sizes such as 256MB, 512MB, 1GB, 5GB, and 16GB and are an easy way to transfer and store information.

Memory Card • An electronic flash memory storage disk commonly used in consumer electronic devices such as digital cameras, MP3 players, mobile phones, and other small portable devices. • Memory cards are usually read by connecting the device containing the card to your computer, or by using a USB card reader.

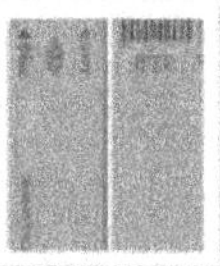

Secure Digital card (SD) MiniSD Compact Flash Memory Stick

MultiMedia card XD-Picture card Memory card reader

Storage Device Features

- Volatility
- Accessibility
- Mutability
- Addressability

Two types of volatility: - Volatile Memory - Non-Volatile Memory

Volatile Memory

- Requires constant power to maintain the stored information.
- The fastest memory technologies.
- All contents are erased when the system's power is turned off or interrupted.
- It has been more popularly known as temporary memory.

Non-Volatile Memory

- Will retain the stored information even if it is not constantly supplied with electric power.
- Nonvolatile memory is the device which keeps the data even when the current is off.
- It is suitable for long-term storage of information.

Accessibility

- Refers to reading or writing data records
- Two types of accessibility: - Random access - Sequential access

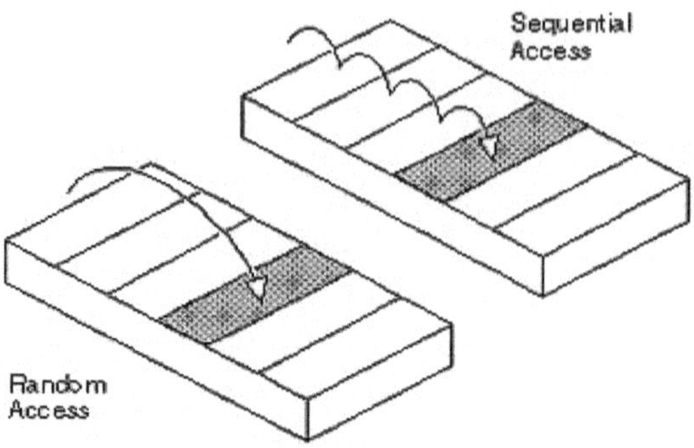

Random Access

• Any location in storage can be accessed at any moment in approximately the same amount of time. • Such characteristic is well suited for primary and secondary storage.

Sequential Access

• The accessing of pieces of information will be in a serial order, one after the other; therefore, the time to access a particular piece of information depends upon which piece of information was last accessed. • Such characteristic is typical of off-line storage.

Mutability

• Allows information to be overwritten at any time.

• A computer without some amount of read/write storage for primary storage purposes would be useless for many tasks.

• Three types of mutability: – Read/write storage or mutable storage – Read only storage – Slow write, fast read storage.

Read/Write Storage or Mutable Storage

• Allows information to be overwritten at any time.

• A computer without some amount of read/write storage for primary storage purposes would be useless for many tasks.

Read Only Storage

• Retains the information stored at the time of manufacture, and write once storage (WORM) allows the information to be written only once at some point after manufacture.

• These are called immutable storage.

Slow Write, Fast Read Storage

• Read/write storage which allows information to be overwritten multiple times, but with the write operation being much slower than the read operation.

Addressability

• Three types of addressability – Location-addressable – File addressable – Content-addressable

Location-addressable

• Each individually accessible unit of information in storage is selected with its numerical memory address.

File addressable

• Information is divided into files of variable length, and a particular file is selected with human-readable directory and file names.

Content-addressable

• Each individually accessible unit of information is selected based on the basis of (part of) the contents stored there.

• Content-addressable storage can be implemented using software (computer program) or hardware (computer device), with hardware being faster but more expensive option.

• Hardware content addressable memory is often used in a computer's CPU cache.

Other Example of Storage Devices

• Punch card • Cloud storage

Punched Card

• Early method of data storage used with early computers

• Punch cards also known as Hollerith cards

• Containing several punched holes that represents data

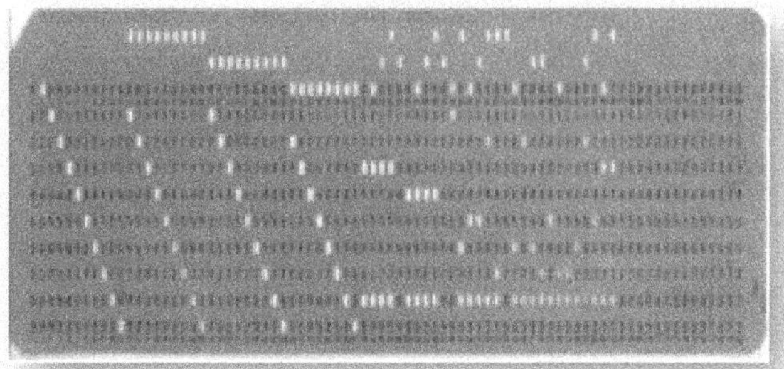

Cloud Storage

• Cloud storage means "the storage of data online in the cloud," wherein a data is stored in and accessible from multiple distributed and connected resources that comprise a cloud.

• Cloud storage can provide the benefits of greater accessibility and reliability; rapid deployment; strong protection for data backup, archival and disaster recovery purposes.

Cloud Storage • Examples: – Google Drive – Flickr – Microsoft Sky Drive

2.3 Computer Software: System Software, Application Software and Utility Software.

Computer Software:

A software or computer software essentially a type of programs which enable the users to perform some particular specific tasks or actually used to operate their computer. It essentially directs all of the peripheral devices on the entire computer system- what exactly to do and how exactly to perform a task. A software plays a key role of a mediator between the user and the computer hardware. In the absence of software, a user essentially can't perform any task on a computer.

What is System Software?

System Software is a set of programs that manage and control the operation of a computer system and its associated devices. It is responsible for allocating system resources, ensuring that the hardware and software components of the system work together, and providing an interface for users, applications, and other systems.

Examples of System Software include operating systems, device drivers, compilers, file, and disk management utilities, system libraries, and system services.

Types of System Software

System Software is computer software designed to provide services to users by managing the hardware and software resources of a computer system. It includes operating systems, device drivers, utilities, firmware, and middleware.

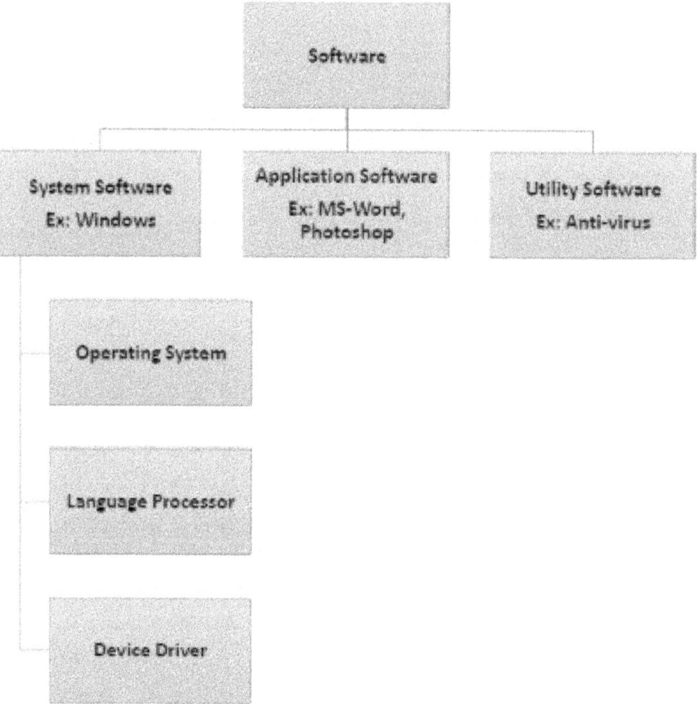

Based on its function, system software is of following types

- Operating System
- Language Processor
- Device Drivers

Operating System

Operating systems are computer System Software responsible for managing the hardware and software resources of a computer system. Examples include Windows, Linux, macOS, iOS, and Android.

System software that is responsible for functioning of all hardware parts and their interoperability to carry out tasks successfully is called **operating system (OS)**. OS is the first software to be loaded into computer memory when the computer is switched on and this is called **booting**. OS manages a computer's basic functions like storing data in memory, retrieving files from storage devices, scheduling tasks based on priority, etc.

Language Processor

As discussed earlier, an important function of system software is to convert all user instructions into machine understandable language. When we talk of human machine interactions, languages are of three types –

- **Machine-level language** – This language is nothing but a string of 0s and 1s that the machines can understand. It is completely machine dependent.
- **Assembly-level language** – This language introduces a layer of abstraction by defining **mnemonics**. **Mnemonics** are English like words or symbols used to denote a long string of 0s and 1s. For example, the word "READ" can be defined to mean that computer has to retrieve data from the memory. The complete **instruction** will also tell the memory address. Assembly level language is **machine dependent**.
- **High level language** – This language uses English like statements and is completely independent of machines. Programs written using high level languages are easy to create, read and understand.

Program written in high level programming languages like Java, C++, etc. is called **source code**. Set of instructions in machine readable form is called **object code** or **machine code**. **System software** that converts source code to object code is called **language processor**. There are three types of language interpreters–

- **Assembler** – Converts assembly level program into machine level program.
- **Interpreter** – Converts high level programs into machine level program line by line.
- **Compiler** – Converts high level programs into machine level programs at one go rather than line by line.

Device Drivers

System software that controls and monitors functioning of a specific device on computer is called **device driver**. Each device like printer, scanner, microphone, speaker, etc. that needs to be attached externally to the system has a specific driver associated with it. When you attach a new device, you need to install its driver so that the OS knows how it needs to be managed.

Functions of System Software

- System Software is a set of instructions and programs that control the operations of a computer system. It is the most basic form of software and is essential for any computer system to function properly.
- System Software performs a variety of tasks, including managing system resources, such as memory, disk space, and processor time. It also provides system interfaces, allowing applications to interact with the hardware. System Software also coordinates the activities of the user, the application, and the hardware.

The main functions of System Software include:

- **Operating System:**

An operating system is a set of programs that manage the resources of a computer and provides an interface for users to interact with the computer. It is responsible for managing the hardware and software components of a system.

- **Device Drivers:**
  Device drivers are software programs that enable hardware devices, such as printers and scanners, to communicate with the operating system.
- **Utility Programs:**
  Utility programs are programs that are used to perform specific tasks, such as disk defragmentation, disk repair, file compression, and virus protection.

II-Application Software:

Application software is a type of software designed to perform specific user tasks, such as word processing, spreadsheet creation, and image editing.

Features of System Software

System Software is software that manages and controls the hardware and other software on a computer system. Some common features of System Software include:

- **Memory management:**
  System Software manages the allocation and deallocation of memory for different programs and processes.
- **Process management:**
  System Software controls the execution of different processes and manages their interactions.
- **Input/Output management:**
  System Software manages the communication between the computer and its various input and output devices, such as the keyboard, mouse, and monitor.
- **File management:**
  System Software controls the organization and storage of files on the computer's hard drive.
- **Security**:
  System Software includes security features such as firewalls and antivirus programs to protect the computer from malware and other malicious software.

- **Device drivers**:
  System Software includes device drivers, which are specialized programs that allow the computer to communicate with specific hardware devices.
- **Networking**:
  System Software includes networking features that allow the computer to connect to other computers and devices on network.
- **Scheduling:**
  System Software schedules tasks to be performed at specific times or under specific conditions.
- **Utilities:**
  System Software includes various utilities such as a defragmenter, disk cleanup, and backup software.

System Software Examples

There are many different types of System Software, including:

- **Operating systems:**
  Operating systems, such as Windows, macOS, and Linux, are the most basic type of System Software. They manage the overall operation of the computer, including memory management, process management, and input/output management.
- **Device drivers:**
  Device drivers are specialized software programs that allow the computer to communicate with specific hardware devices, such as printers, keyboards, and hard drives.
- **Firmware:**
  Firmware is low-level software that controls specific hardware components, such as BIOS or UEFI in a computer's motherboard.
- **File systems:**
  File systems, such as NTFS and FAT32, are responsible for organizing and storing files on the computer's hard drive.

- **Utilities**:
  Utilities are small programs that perform specific functions, such as disk cleanup, defragmenting, and backup software.
- **Virtualization software:**
  Virtualization software, such as VMware and Hyper-V, allows multiple operating systems to run on one physical computer, creating virtual machines.
- **Antivirus and security software:**
  Antivirus and security software, such as McAfee and Norton, protect the computer from malware and other malicious software.
- **Networking software:**
  Networking software, such as TCP/IP and DHCP, enables the communication between computers and other devices on a network.
- **Backup and recovery software:**
  Backup and recovery software, such as Acronis and Norton Ghost, allows users to backup and restore their files and system settings.

Uses of System Software

System Software is used for a variety of purposes, including:

- **Managing and controlling the overall operation of a computer:**
  Operating systems, such as Windows, macOS, and Linux, are responsible for managing the computer's memory, processing power, and input/output devices.
- **Communicating with hardware devices:**
  Device drivers allow the computer to communicate with specific hardware devices, such as printers, keyboards, and hard drives.
- **Storing and organizing files:**
  File systems, such as NTFS and FAT32, are responsible for organizing and storing files on the computer's hard drive.
- **Enhancing security:**
  Antivirus and security software, such as McAfee and Norton, protect the computer from malware and other malicious

software, and firewalls protect the computer from unauthorized access.

- **Facilitating communication with other devices:**
  Networking software, such as TCP/IP and DHCP, enables communication between computers and other devices on a network.
- **Performing system maintenance:**
  Utilities, such as disk cleanup, defragmenting, and backup software, are used to perform various system maintenance tasks.
- **Virtualizing the physical resources:**
  Virtualization software, such as VMware and Hyper-V, allows multiple operating systems to run on one physical computer, creating virtual machines.
- **Allowing remote access and control:**
  Remote access software, such as TeamViewer and Remote Desktop, allows users to remotely access and control other computers.
- **Facilitating development and testing:**
  System Software such as debuggers, profilers, and emulators are used by developers and testers to test and debug their code.
- **Managing resources and scheduling tasks:**
  Scheduling software is used to schedule tasks to be performed at specific times or under specific conditions.

III- Utility Software

- The Utility Software is system software that helps to maintain the proper and smooth functioning of a Computer System. It assists the Operating System to manage, organize, maintain, and optimize the functioning of the computer system.
- Utility Software performs certain tasks like virus detection, installation, and uninstallation, data backup, deletion of unwanted files, etc. Some examples are antivirus software, file management tools, compression tools, disk management tools, etc.

Types of Utility Software

1. Antivirus

- A virus is a malicious software that enters the system along with a host program. Moreover, it multiplies with time and makes several copies which in turn slows down and corrupts the system.
- An antivirus is a utility software that helps to keep the computer virus-free. Moreover, it notifies when any malicious file is detected and removes such files. In addition, it scans any new device attached to the computer and discards any virus if there. Moreover, it also scans the system from time to time for any threats and disposes of them. Examples of antivirus are McAfee Antivirus, Quickheal Antivirus, Windows Defender, etc.

2. File Management System

- This utility software is used to manage files of the computer system. Since files are an important part of the system as all the data is stored in the files. Therefore, this utility software help to browse, search, arrange, find information, and quickly preview the files of the system.
- Windows Explorer is a default file management tool present in the system. Some other examples of file management tools are Google Desktop, Double Commander, Directory Opus, etc.

3. Compression Tools

- An important part of a computer is storage space, it is very important to maintain this storage. Therefore, we use certain utility software to compress big files and decrease their size, these are compression tools.The format of the files changes while compressing and we cannot access or edit them directly. In addition, we can easily decompress the file and get the original file back. Examples of compression tools are WinZip, WinRAR, WinAce, PeaZip, 7-Zip, etc.

4. Disk Management Tools

- This utility software are used to manage data on disks. Moreover, they perform functions like partitioning devices, manage drives, etc. Examples of disk management tools are MiniTool Partition Wizard, Paragon Partition Manager, etc.

5. Disk Cleanup Tool

- This utility software helps to free up the disk space. In addition, the files which are no longer in use are removed from the disk. Examples are Razer Cortex, Piriform CCleaner, etc.

6. Disk Defragmenter

- This utility software helps to reduce the fragmentation and hence, reduces the access speed. Defragmenting refers to rearranging files and storing them in contiguous memory locations. Moreover, saves time in reading from files and writing files to disk. Examples of disk defragmenters are Perfect disk, Deflaggler, etc.

7. Backup Utility

- This utility software helps to back up the files, folders, databases, or complete disks. Moreover, backup refers to duplicating the disk information so that the data can be restored if any data loss happens.

2.4 Application of word processing software in Education: Microsoft Word, Google Docs, WPS Word.

One of the most widely used programs of Microsoft Office suite, MS Word is a word processor developed by Microsoft. An introduction to MS Word, its features and its uses, have all been discussed in detail, in this article. Also, a few sample questions based on this MS Office program have been given further below for the reference of candidates preparing for competitive exams. To know further about the MS Office suite and the various programs included in it, visit the linked article.

Microsoft Word

Since MS Word is one of the most used programs of the Office Suite, some basic information regarding its creation and development has been given below:

- Charles Simonyi, a developer and Richard Brodie, a software engineer, were the two creators of MS Word
- This program was initially named "multi-Tool Word" but later, was renamed as MS Word
- It was introduced in 1983

- Word for Windows is available standalone or as a part of MS Office suite
- MS Word for Mac was introduced by Microsoft as Word 1.0 in 1985
- The extension for any word file is ".doc or .docx."

Moving forward, details about the features and applications of Word have been discussed. To read more about the other Computer Knowledge topics, check the links given below:

Basics of MS Word

Let us first understand some basic aspects of Microsoft Word.

What is MS Word?

Used to make professional-quality documents, letters, reports, etc., MS Word is a word processor developed by Microsoft. It has advanced features which allow you to format and edit your files and documents in the best possible way.

What are the uses of MS Word?

MS Word enables users to do write-ups, create documents, resumes, contracts, etc. This is one of the most commonly used programs under the Office suite.

How to create an MS Word document?

To create an MS Word doc, follow the steps mentioned above to open Microsoft Word. Then once the program is open, click on "File" followed by "New". This opens a new doc where something new can be created.

Since it is used by people of all age groups, in schools, in colleges and for official purposes, having proper knowledge of Microsoft Word is a must. The preview of the MS Doc file once it is opened is given below:

Features of MS Word

Now let us read more about the features and components of an MS Word doc file in detail.

The image given below shows the different elements and categories which are available in MS Word doc:

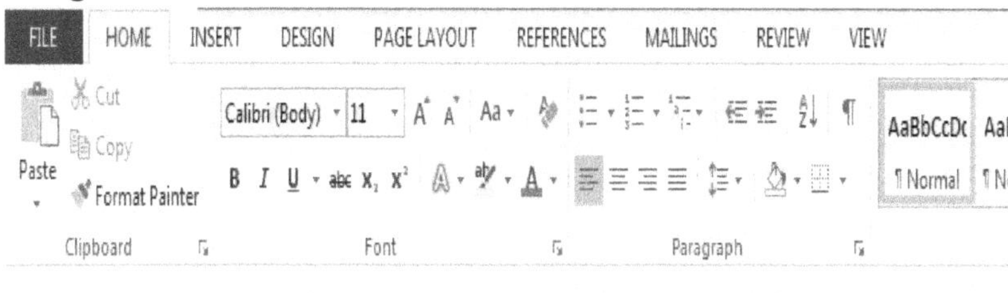

- **Home**

  This has options like font color, font size, font style, alignment, bullets, line spacing, etc. All the basic elements which one may need to edit their document is available under the home option.
- **Insert**

  Tables, shapes, images, charts, graphs, header, footer, page number, etc. can all be entered in the document. They are included in the "Insert" category.
- **Design**

  The template or the design in which you want your document to be created can be selected under the Design tab. Choosing an appropriate tab will enhance the appearance of your document.
- **Page Layout**

  Under the Page Layout tab comes options like margins, orientation, columns, lines, indentation, spacing, etc.
- **References**

  This tab is the most useful for those who are creating a thesis or writing books or lengthy documents. Options like citation, footnote, table of contents, caption, bibliography, etc. can be found under this tab.
- **Review**

  Spell check, grammar, Thesaurus, word count, language, translation, comments, etc. can all be tracked under the review tab. This acts as an advantage for those who get their documents reviewed on MS Word.

Apart from all the above-mentioned features, the page can be set in different views and layouts, which can be added and optimized using the View tab on the Word document. Margins and scales are also available for the benefit of the users.

When compared with MS PowerPoint, MS Word is more of reading while PPT is more of visual and graphical representation of data.

Uses of MS Word

Given below are the different fields in which MS Word is used and simplifies the work of an individual:

- **In Education:** It is considered as one of the simplest tools which can be used by both teachers and students. Creating notes is easier using MS Word as they can be made more interactive by adding shapes and images. It is also convenient to make assignments on MS Word and submitting them online
- **In Workplace:** Submitting letters, bills, creating reports, letterheads, sample documents, can all easily be done using MS Word
- **Creating & Updating Resume:** One of the best tools to create your resumes and is easy to edit and make changes in it as per your experience
- **For Authors:** Since separate options are available for bibliography, table of contents, etc., it is the best tool which can be used by authors for writing books and adjusting it as per the layout and alignment of your choice

Google Docs

- Google Docs is one of the most sophisticated yet user-friendly tools created by Google Inc., the multinational technology enterprise. With the advent of technology, fast-paced lives, shorter deadlines, and the need to give and receive instant feedback, sending documents to a team member sitting across the globe and then waiting for them to respond has become obsolete. Back in the day, only one person at a time could check out a document on a server so as to maintain versions. Not anymore.

- With Google Docs, team members working across the world can now collaborate, write, edit, comment, and resolve issues instantaneously. All that is needed is a registered Gmail ID. If there's more than one person whose inputs are required, then all such collaborators can be 'tagged' on the document with the help of a '@' sign and made a comment to. These collaborators then will get a notification and those can be resolved instantaneously.
- Google Docs is a Web-based document management application for creating and editing private and public, word processing and spreadsheet documents. These documents can be stored both online on the Google cloud and/or on the user's computer. Access to these files is available from any computer with an Internet connection and a fully-featured Web browser. The documents may be viewed by other google groups and members with the document owner's permission.
- Google Docs is designed for both individual and real-time collaborative projects. Document security is maintained through storage online and storage on users' computers, although some authors have security concerns that documents stored online may be viewed, copied or stolen by others. Furthermore, all documents created are compatible with most presentation and word processing applications and can be printed or published as a Web page. Spreadsheets can be created and edited in various fonts and file formats.

Google Docs enables user to perform the following:

- Create and share documents on the web and access them from any computer or smart phone. The familiar desktop feel makes collaborative editing easy.
- Share and collaborate instantly
- Invite anyone to edit and collaborate on your spreadsheet.
- Store files online

- Publish to the world, just a few people or no one -- it's up to you. You can also un–publish at any time.

Google Docs uses.

- Google Docs is an easy-to-use, web-based application that requires a Google account. The same Google account credentials can be used to access and work on Google Docs. It can be accessed using https://docs.google.com/ or through Google Drive https://drive.google.com/. The New->Google Docs option opens a new Google Docs document.
- It can be shared using a link or an email to a person or a group of people in the class. If it's a document that's shared with all, then everyone can access it at the same time and can view and edit it. Comments can be left on the same document for others to contribute or resolve issues.
- This ready-to-use, automatically saved document has the same tools as a system-installed Microsoft Office Word document.
- Because of the web-based, real-time, collaborative nature of the tool, Google Docs works very well for students. Moreover, it's free. The only requirement for using Google Docs is a registered Gmail ID. It's safe to use as only the teacher and students who have access to view or edit this document can access it. Students can work on the same document as the teacher and at the same time. Students can get their assignments reviewed fast and with minimal wait time. Also, students don't need a separate software to work while at school or at home.
- As a student, Google Docs can be used to create documents from scratch, work on the assigned documents and tasks, fill worksheets, review, and edit documents as an individual student or as a team for a group project. While collaborating on a team project, students can leave comments for each other that helps resolve issues in the quickest manner possible.

- It can also be used to review self-graded assignments and learn from mistakes without having to wait for feedback from the teacher. The results are instantaneously received.

Google Docs in the Classroom.

Google Docs for school is a boon for the student community. It has easy-to-use features that let the students collaborate, take notes, create and revise documents as a team. The result is instantaneous. Any number of students or teachers can view, edit, or make any number of suggestions to the document at the same time from any location. This saves time, provides instant, real-time feedback, and helps resolve queries or issues in the document quickly.

Even if the student goes offline for a few minutes, they can continue to work on the same document. The next time they come online, the document gets updated and synced with the latest version from the cloud.

Google Docs for Students

- Google Docs is more than just a word processing tool. It has the editing tools to add line spacing for better legibility, change and select fonts, headers, footers, columns, rows, and tables to organize data and the power to access it from anywhere. Documents can be started in one location and finished in another. The cloud which is called Google Drive helps store and retrieve it, irrespective of time and location.
- Documents thus stored can be organized by owner, last modified date, or file size. Folders are extremely helpful in organizing tasks and documents. The same files or folders can be easily shared with other collaborators, such as peer reviewers and teachers. The file or folder can be shared using a link that can be copied or sent to their email id. The levels of permission can be easily controlled by the owner of the document, from view being the least to edit and comment being the most.

- Google Docs also provides the option of downloading a copy of the document to the local system in any of the available formats, such as PDF, TXT, HTML, etc. The *Explore* option lets the user search for relevant images or sources from the Internet and add them to the document. Google Docs provides several templates to create reports, essays, class notes, presentations, etc. Using convenient voice typing, students can type an entire essay without having to touch the keyboard. The translation feature helps translate the document from a source language to a target language without fuss.

WPS Word.

Word Processing System or WPS Office Software, abbreviated as WPS, has gained immense popularity among professionals and students within less time. A survey concludes that the popularity of the WPS office has reached almost six hundred million monthly active users and more than one billion installations.

What is WPS?

A WPS Office is an office suite that gives the user access to word, presentation, and Excel files. It is an easy-to-use tool that is compatible with almost every device and operating system. You can use it with Microsoft Windows, macOS, Linux, iOS, Android, and Harmony OS, thus making it one of the highly recommended software for maintaining data.

Essential components of WPS Office:

The three essential components of the WPS office are:

1. WPS Writer- it is used for making assignments and reports.
2. WPS Presentation- the user can make multi-media presentations for official meetings or final projects.
3. WPS Spreadsheet- the excel sheet is used to keep a record of various kinds of data, and the user can access it within no time.

Valuable Features of WPS Office for students:

Heavy college bags, books, and laptops make it difficult for students to manage life within and out of campus. Situations become tougher when a student, by any chance, loses his important academic file. The double mental and physical burden makes their day more exhausting. For this purpose, the WPS Office has launched equally beneficial features for students. These features have helped the students quickly get over their academic tasks and presentations and carry their essential data anywhere.

The following features of the WPS Office are specially designed and added for the convenience of students, teachers, and other professionals. Let's have a look:

1. Text Tools:

- With the text tools, the students can store and organize a large amount of data. They can also copy a large amount of text from the webpage and paste that in multiple layouts and sizes into WPS.
- With WPS, just a single click (Home- Text Tools- Smart Rearrange) allows the user to format the contents of documents in a designed format. The word processor of the WPS Office is featured with a drag-and-drop, enabling students to adjust line and paragraph spacing according to their task requirements. The editing of documents is also easy. It saves time for students.

2. Online template:

The next feature is the WPS online template. The students can mix text, graphics, pictures, and other subjects with this online template. Instead of extended bland mix and match procedures, the online template makes tasks more accessible and interesting for the students.

3. Take photos and scan them:

Taking photos with the camera and scanning them for various purposes is not an easy job. With WPS Office, the students can take pictures and scan the entire page. A PDF file is generated that they can review later.

Most students find it useful for reading e-books. The students can download the e-books in PDF format that they can read on any device.

4. PDF Tools:

With the PDF tools, the students can easily access PDF to DOC, PDF Edit, PDF Add Text, and many other PDF features. They can save the PDF file for later use.

The students can also convert word documents into PDF files. Converting large documents into smaller PDF files makes it easier for file sharing with other fellows and teachers.

5. Make presentations:

Presentations are an essential part of a student's curriculum. While most students find it hard, many find it easy because they use the WPS Office.

With the PPT Recorder, the students can record the playback process of the PowerPoint Presentation itself. The PPT Recorder records the speaker's voice, automatically turns the slides or pages, and all screens are recorded and stored in an MP4 format.

Moreover, with the already available PPT templates on this software, the students can make presentations within minutes. The general presentation templates allow inserting different multi-media, including images, audio, and videos. Making presentations was never that easier without the WPS Office.

6. File Recovery:

With this feature, the students can recover their deleted word documents, excel sheets, or PDF files. The WPS Data Recovery Master allows them to conduct a deep data recovery.

7. Processing complex data:

Students often have to calculate complex data in their Finance subjects. For this purpose, every time, they have to expand the cells. One of the best functions of the WPS Office is that the WPS Spreadsheet automatically processes the fed data long data, thus making the data intuitive. The WPS Office simplifies the students' complex operational steps and saves them time.

8. WPS Cloud:

- The WPS Cloud makes it an outstanding software for many. WPS Cloud can store all kinds of files, including Words files, excel spreadsheets, videos, photos, PDF files, and audio. The WPS Cloud is considered a Flash drive that carries your essential documents along with you. It can store up to 20 GB.
- The features also ensure that the students can access all their essential documents from any device. For instance, if a student has made a presentation on his PC and stored it in his WPS office, he can also access it using his university computer lab's computer. Thus, the WPS Cloud has made data synchronization much easier for everyone.
- A modern student involves and interacts with other students plus teachers, participates in classroom discussions, and acts in a receptive manner, with the unique feature of WPS, called Students Tool. Considering the needs of modern organizations, how can WPS overlook the students? Students and their current educational requirements are the most critical assets of any society or economy.

2.5 Application of spread sheet software in Education: Microsoft Excel, Google Sheets.

Microsoft Excel

MS Excel is a commonly used Microsoft Office application. It is a spreadsheet program which is used to save and analyse numerical data.

In this article, we bring to you the important features of MS Excel, along with an overview of how to use the program, its benefits and other important elements. A few samples MS Excel question and answers are also given further below in this article for the reference of Government exam aspirants.

Basics of MS Excel

What is MS Excel?

MS Excel is a spreadsheet program where one can record data in the form of tables. It is easy to analyse data in an Excel spreadsheet. The image given below represents how an Excel spreadsheet looks like:

It is easy to analyse data in an Excel spreadsheet. The image given below represents how an Excel spreadsheet looks like:

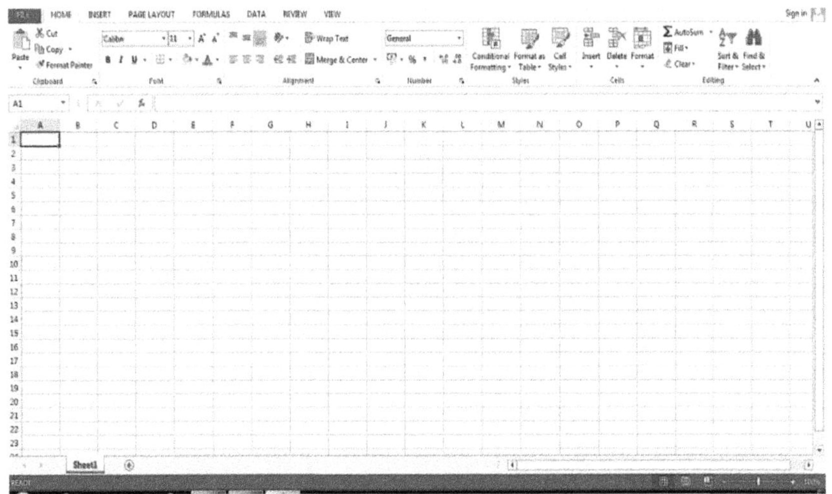

How to open MS Excel?

To open MS Excel on your computer, follow the steps given below:

- Click on Start
- Then All Programs
- Next step is to click on MS Office
- Then finally, choose the MS-Excel option

Alternatively, you can also click on the Start button and type MS Excel in the search option available.

What is a cell?

A spreadsheet is in the form of a table comprising rows and columns. The rectangular box at the intersection point between rows and columns forms a cell. Given below is an image of a cell:

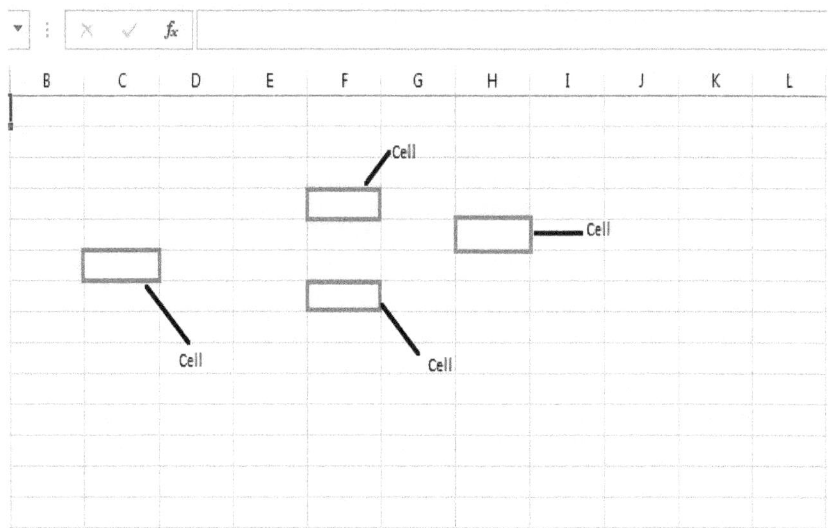

What is Cell Address?

The cell address is the name by which is cell can be addressed. For example, if row 7 is interested in column G, then the cell address is G7.

Features of MS Excel

Various editing and formatting can be done on an Excel spreadsheet. Discussed below are the various features of MS Excel.

The image below shows the composition of features in MS Excel:

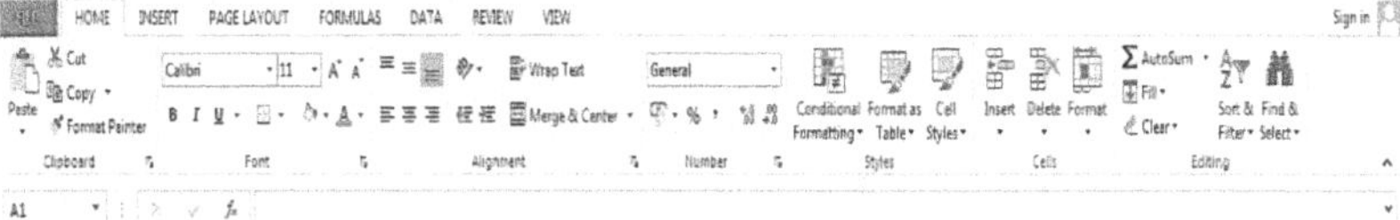

- **Home**

  Comprises options like font size, font styles, font colour, background colour, alignment, formatting options and styles, insertion and deletion of cells and editing options

- **Insert**

  Comprises options like table format and style, inserting images and figures, adding graphs, charts and sparklines, header and footer option, equation and symbols

- **Page Layout**
  Themes, orientation and page setup options are available under the page layout option
- **Formulas**
  Since tables with a large amount of data can be created in MS excel, under this feature, you can add formulas to your table and get quicker solutions
- **Data**
  Adding external data (from the web), filtering options and data tools are available under this category
- **Review**
  Proofreading can be done for an excel sheet (like spell check) in the review category and a reader can add comments in this part
- **View**
  Different views in which we want the spreadsheet to be displayed can be edited here. Options to zoom in and out and pane arrangement are available under this category

Benefits of Using MS Excel

MS Excel is widely used for various purposes because the data is easy to save, and information can be added and removed without any discomfort and less hard work.

Given below are a few important benefits of using MS Excel:

- **Easy To Store Data:** Since there is no limit to the amount of information that can be saved in a spreadsheet, MS Excel is widely used to save data or to analyse data. Filtering information in Excel is easy and convenient.
- **Easy To Recover Data:** If the information is written on a piece of paper, finding it may take longer, however, this is not the case with excel spreadsheets. Finding and recovering data is easy.
- **Application of Mathematical Formulas:** Doing calculations has become easier and less time-taking with the formulas option in MS excel
- **More Secure:** These spreadsheets can be password secured in a laptop or personal computer and the

probability of losing them is way lesser in comparison to data written in registers or piece of paper.

- **Data at One Place:** Earlier, data was to be kept in different files and registers when the paperwork was done. Now, this has become convenient as more than one worksheet can be added in a single MS Excel file.
- **Neater and Clearer Visibility of Information:** When the data is saved in the form of a table, analysing it becomes easier. Thus, information is a spreadsheet that is more readable and understandable.

MS Excel – Points to Remember

There are certain things which one must know with respect to MS Excel, its applications and usage:

- An MS Excel file is saved with an extension of .xls
- Companies with large staff and workers use MS Excel as saving employee information becomes easier
- Excel spreadsheets are also used in hospitals where the information of patients can be saved more easily and can be removed conveniently once their medical history is cleared
- The sheet on which you work is called a Worksheet
- Multiple worksheets can be added in a single Excel file
- This is a data processing application
- **Google Sheets**.
- Google Sheets is an online spreadsheet software known for its collaboration, while Microsoft Excel is desktop software that manages large data sets and complex computations. Both are well-known and can aid in many facets of business, like forecasting future performance, calculating taxes or revenues, aiding in payroll functions, and creating charts.
- While both Google Sheets and Microsoft Excel give users the ability to create and manage spreadsheets, each has its strengths and weaknesses. This article explores those differences in greater detail to help you decide on the option that will work best for you.

- Google Sheets is a web-based application that provides users access to seamless collaboration or solo creation, editing, and management of spreadsheets from their browser. The spreadsheet solution, which launched in 2006 and is part of Google's G Suite, is free and easy to use.
- Google Sheets offers simultaneous collaboration, which means multiple people from different locations can edit the spreadsheet with information updated in real time.

While collaboration is one of its biggest perks, Google Sheets offers the day-to-day functionality that users typically need. With Google Sheets, users can:

- Create, edit, format, and save spreadsheets online
- Apply formulas and functions to data sets
- Visualize spreadsheet data in basic charts or graphs
- Share documents and folders with multiple users
- Import spreadsheets into other file formats like Google Docs or Microsoft Word

Who uses Google Sheets?

Since the software is free, students, teachers, and small businesses often turn to Google Sheets for their spreadsheet needs. Additionally, its collaboration features set it apart, making it preferred by many small teams that need to collaborate or companies that rely heavily on remote workers. With team members working in different countries and time zones, Google Sheets gives everyone a chance to work together in their own time frame. Remote teams tend to rely on other Google tools, including Google Meet, Slides, and Docs, so working within one suite of tools makes sense.

The following image represents the primary interface of Google sheets, which is the typical screen we see for the first time when creating a new sheet:

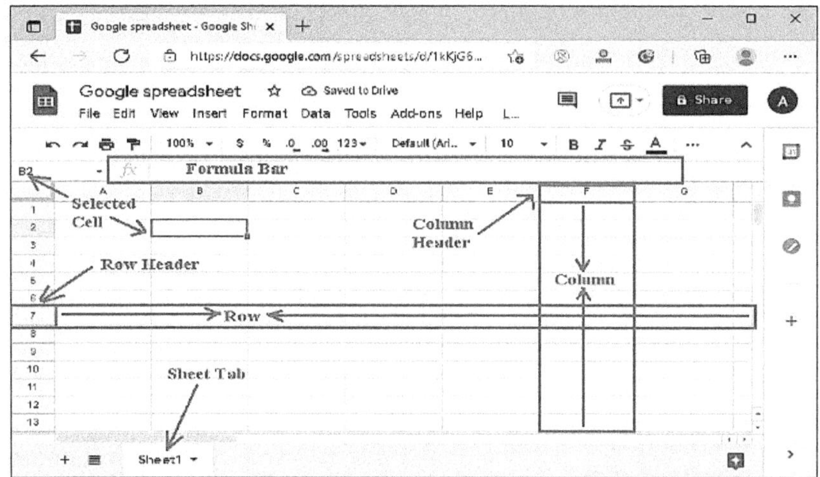

Advantages

- Easy to use
- Free to use
- Inbuilt real-time revision history with chat support
- Excellent visibility and rigid integration with Google
- Better sharing support with no version compatibility issues
- Supports an extensive range of add-ons and Google other products

Disadvantages

- Becomes slow with the vast amounts of data
- Supports limited formulae and functions
- Limited options for data visualization and customizations
- Key Differences between Excel and Google Sheets
- The following are some key differences between the MS Excel and Google sheets:
- MS Excel is included with the MS Office suite, whereas Google sheets is a part of the G Suite (Google suite).
- MS Excel is expensive, and its latest version (Office 365 Excel Online) charges a monthly or yearly fee, depending on the user's selection. Besides, Google Sheets is entirely free for personal use and only requires a Google Account.

- MS Excel supports over 400 functions/ formulae, while Google sheets has limited options.
- MS Excel deals with complex tasks and large data sets efficiently. On the other hand, Google sheets is more suited for basic operations and small data sets.
- MS Excel (except Office 365) does not have a collaboration feature, and it asks users to save their files first to send/share them with others. On the other hand, Google Sheets is an entirely web-based tool, and hence, it allows users to share sheets with others and work together in real-time.
- Data analysis is more straightforward and effective in MS Excel as it can handle vast amounts of data. Besides, Google sheets is not usually made for data analysis. Instead, it is the data entry tool developed for performing basic spreadsheet tasks.
- MS Excel is best suited for large-scale companies or businesses. In contrast, Google sheets is best suited for freelancers, students, and small companies.

UNIT 3: EDUCATIONAL AIMS AND OBJECTIVES

3.1-Educational aims: meaning, importance, factors determining educational aims.

- Education is a purposeful and ethical activity and each activity as aspect has some aim before it. So, there is a close relationship between an activity and its aim.
- An aim is a conscious purpose which we set before us, while launching upon any activity. Just like that education is also unthinkable without aims. If there are no aims the educational process would not take place because an aim is a pre-determined goal which inspires the activity of education.
- Aims act as basic directions while conducting research or carrying out a project. It can be chunked into various objectives which help in reaching the aim easily. It has a long-range perspective which reflects aspirations and ambition of the entity.
- In the words of John Dewey "An aim is a foreseen end that gives direction to an activity or motivates behavior".

Importance of Educational Aims

All our methods of teaching, our curriculum and our system of evaluation are shaped and molded according to our aim of education. It is the ignorance of right aims that has vitiated our educational system, its methods and its products, and has successfully resulted in the physical, intellectual and moral weaknesses of the race. There is a great necessity of aims in education because of the following reasons:

1.To direct efforts: Educational aims keep the teacher and the taught on the right track. They provide a line of action and guidance to the teachers. They give direction and zest to the work of the pupils. Educational aims help us to avoid wastage in time and energy.

2.To evaluate ourselves: The aim is a yard-stick with which we can measure our success and failure. They are necessary to assess the outcome of the educational process.

3. **To provide efficient** administration : Aims are necessary for efficient school administration and organization. They help the school authorities in organizing, equipping, and administering the school.

Factors determining Educational Aims

Many factors have been contributing and do contribute to the determining of educational aims. These factors touch every phase of human life that was, that is or what will be.

1.**Factors associated with Philosophy of life**: Aims of education are always influenced by the philosophy of life of the people of that country.

2. **Factors associated with Psychology**: The aims of education should be according to the nature, needs, requirements, inspiration and interest of the learners. The aims of education should relate knowledge with the activities of life.

3. **Factors associated with Socio-economic problem**: Besides, political ideologies, the social economic problems of a country, determine the aims of education

4. **Factors associated with Political ideology:** Political ideologies also help in determining the aims of education. The aims of education are fixed in accordance with the ideology of the state to uphold the right of state.

5. **Factors associated with exploration of knowledge**: Education has also to give due consideration to the advancements in knowledge as for as the question of educational aims are concerned.

6. **Factors associated with Culture**: It is the most important function of the education to develop and preserve the cultural heritage. The changing and developing pattern of cultural factors directly influence the aims of education.

3.2 Educational objectives: meaning, importance, types, characteristics and purpose.

Meaning of Educational Objectives

Educational objectives, also known as learning objectives or instructional objectives, are specific, measurable statements that clearly describe what learners will know, be able to do, or demonstrate as a result of a learning activity or program. These objectives serve as a roadmap for both educators and students, guiding the teaching and learning process.

Importance of Educational Objectives

1. **Clarity and Focus:**
    - Educational objectives provide clarity for both teachers and students by outlining what is expected to be learned. This helps in focusing the teaching efforts and learning activities towards achieving specific outcomes.
2. **Guidance for Instruction:**
    - They serve as a guide for instructors in planning and delivering lessons. By having clear objectives, teachers can design activities, assignments, and assessments that align with the desired learning outcomes.
3. **Assessment and Evaluation:**
    - Well-defined objectives enable the creation of assessments that accurately measure whether students have achieved the desired learning outcomes. This facilitates objective evaluation of student performance.
4. **Student Motivation and Engagement:**
    - When students understand the objectives of their learning, they are more likely to be motivated and engaged. Knowing what is expected helps students set their own goals and take ownership of their learning process.
5. **Curriculum Development:**
    - Educational objectives are crucial in the development and alignment of curricula. They ensure that the curriculum is structured in a way that progressively builds knowledge and skills.
6. **Accountability:**
    - Objectives provide a basis for accountability in education. Teachers, students, and educational institutions can be held accountable for achieving the stated learning outcomes.

7. **Individualized Learning:**
    - Clear objectives help in identifying the individual learning needs of students. Teachers can use these objectives to tailor their instruction to meet the diverse needs of learners.
8. **Continuous Improvement:**
    - Objectives facilitate continuous improvement in education. By evaluating the success of teaching strategies and learning activities against the objectives, educators can make informed decisions about how to enhance the educational process.

Crafting Effective Educational Objectives

Effective educational objectives should be:

1. **Specific:**
    - Clearly define what is to be learned without ambiguity.
2. **Measurable:**
    - Include criteria for assessing whether the learning objective has been achieved.
3. **Achievable:**
    - Be realistic and attainable within the given timeframe and context.
4. **Relevant:**
    - Align with broader educational goals and the needs of the students.
5. **Time-bound:**
    - Specify the time frame within which the objectives should be achieved.

A common framework used to create educational objectives is the SMART criteria (Specific, Measurable, Achievable, Relevant, Time-bound). Additionally, Bloom's Taxonomy provides a hierarchical classification of cognitive skills that can help in developing objectives at various levels of complexity, from basic recall of facts to higher-order thinking skills like analysis and evaluation.

Conclusion

Educational objectives are fundamental to the teaching and learning process. They provide direction, facilitate effective instruction, and enable accurate assessment of student learning. By clearly defining what students are expected to achieve, educational objectives play a critical role in the success of educational programs and the overall development of learners.

Importance of Educational Objectives

Educational objectives are essential in the educational process for several reasons. These objectives provide a clear and structured pathway for both educators and students, ensuring that the learning process is goal-oriented and effective. Below are key reasons highlighting their importance:

1. Guidance and Direction

- **For Educators:** Educational objectives serve as a roadmap, guiding teachers in curriculum development, lesson planning, and instructional methods. They ensure that teaching activities are aligned with desired outcomes.
- **For Students:** Objectives give students a clear understanding of what is expected of them, helping them focus their efforts on achieving specific learning goals.

2. Measurable Outcomes

- **Assessment:** Objectives enable the development of assessments and evaluations that are aligned with the intended learning outcomes. This makes it easier to measure student progress and the effectiveness of instructional methods.
- **Feedback:** Clear objectives provide a basis for meaningful feedback to students, helping them understand their strengths and areas for improvement.

3. Motivation and Engagement

- **Relevance:** When students understand the objectives and see the relevance of what they are learning, they are more likely to be motivated and engaged.

- **Achievement:** Achieving specific objectives can provide students with a sense of accomplishment, boosting their confidence and encouraging further learning.

4. Consistency and Continuity

- **Standardization:** Educational objectives ensure consistency across different classes and educational institutions. This standardization helps maintain a certain level of quality and coherence in education.
- **Progression:** Well-defined objectives facilitate the smooth progression of students from one level of education to the next, ensuring that they build on previously acquired knowledge and skills.

5. Curriculum Development

- **Alignment:** Objectives help in aligning the curriculum with educational standards and societal needs. This ensures that the education system produces individuals who are capable of contributing positively to society.
- **Flexibility:** They provide a framework within which teachers can adapt and innovate, ensuring that the curriculum remains relevant and dynamic.

6. Professional Development

- **Continuous Improvement:** For educators, having clear objectives encourages ongoing professional development. Teachers can assess their teaching strategies against the objectives and seek to improve their instructional techniques.

7. Accountability

- **Responsibility:** Educational objectives hold educators accountable for delivering quality education and achieving specific learning outcomes.
- **Transparency:** They provide a transparent criterion for stakeholders, including parents, administrators, and policymakers, to evaluate the effectiveness of the educational process.

Conclusion

Educational objectives are fundamental to the teaching and learning process. They provide direction, enhance motivation, ensure consistency, and facilitate the measurement of educational outcomes. By establishing clear, achievable goals, educational objectives help create a structured and effective learning environment that benefits both educators and students.

Types of Educational Objectives

Educational objectives can be categorized into different types based on the domain of learning they address and the level of cognitive complexity involved. Understanding these types helps educators design comprehensive curricula and instructional strategies that cater to various aspects of student development. Here are the primary types of educational objectives:

1. Cognitive Objectives

Cognitive objectives relate to the development of intellectual skills and knowledge acquisition. They are often classified using Bloom's Taxonomy, which outlines a hierarchy of cognitive processes.

- **Knowledge:** Recall of facts, terms, basic concepts, or answers.
    - Example: "Students will be able to list the states of the United States."
- **Comprehension:** Understanding of information and the ability to interpret it.
    - Example: "Students will be able to explain the significance of the Bill of Rights."
- **Application:** Use of knowledge in new and concrete situations.
    - Example: "Students will be able to apply the Pythagorean theorem to solve real-world problems."
- **Analysis:** Breaking down information into components and understanding its structure.
    - Example: "Students will be able to analyze the themes of a novel."

- **Synthesis:** Combining elements to form a coherent whole or proposing alternative solutions.
    - Example: "Students will be able to design an experiment to test a scientific hypothesis."
- **Evaluation:** Making judgments based on criteria and standards.
    - Example: "Students will be able to evaluate the effectiveness of different government policies."

2. Affective Objectives

Affective objectives focus on the development of attitudes, values, and feelings. These objectives are crucial for shaping students' emotional and social growth.

- **Receiving:** Awareness, willingness to hear, and selected attention.
    - Example: "Students will be willing to listen to differing viewpoints in a discussion."
- **Responding:** Active participation through reaction or response.
    - Example: "Students will participate in classroom discussions on ethical issues."
- **Valuing:** The worth or value a person attaches to a particular object, phenomenon, or behavior.
    - Example: "Students will demonstrate a commitment to environmental conservation."
- **Organization:** Integrating new values into one's existing value system and prioritizing values.
    - Example: "Students will be able to prioritize their study time over leisure activities."
- **Characterization:** Acting consistently with the new value or attitude.
    - Example: "Students will consistently exhibit honesty in their academic work."

3. Psychomotor Objectives

Psychomotor objectives relate to the development of physical skills and the ability to perform tasks requiring bodily coordination.

- **Perception:** Use of sensory cues to guide motor activity.
    - Example: "Students will be able to identify the correct tools needed for a woodshop project."
- **Set:** Readiness to act, including mental, physical, and emotional dispositions.
    - Example: "Students will demonstrate readiness to perform a musical piece."
- **Guided Response:** Early stages of learning a complex skill, usually under guidance.
    - Example: "Students will perform a basic dance routine under the instructor's guidance."
- **Mechanism:** Intermediate stage of learning where movements are habitual and performance is more proficient.
    - Example: "Students will be able to type at a speed of 40 words per minute with accuracy."
- **Complex Overt Response:** Skillful performance of complex movements.
    - Example: "Students will perform a complex gymnastics routine with precision."
- **Adaptation:** Skills are well developed, and the individual can modify movement patterns to fit special requirements.
    - Example: "Students will adapt a learned welding technique to new and different materials."
- **Origination:** Creating new movement patterns to fit a particular situation or problem.
    - Example: "Students will choreograph a unique dance performance."

Conclusion

Understanding the various types of educational objectives helps educators create a balanced and effective curriculum that addresses cognitive, affective, and psychomotor domains. This comprehensive approach ensures that students develop a well-rounded skill set, encompassing knowledge, attitudes, and physical abilities. By aligning instructional strategies and assessment methods with these objectives, educators can facilitate meaningful and holistic student development.

Characteristics of Educational Objectives

Educational objectives are statements that define the specific learning outcomes educators aim for students to achieve. Effective educational objectives share several key characteristics:

1. **Clarity**
   - **Specific:** Objectives should be clear and specific, leaving no ambiguity about what is expected.
     - Example: Instead of saying "understand photosynthesis," a clearer objective is "describe the process of photosynthesis and explain its importance to plant life."
   - **Concrete:** They should describe observable and measurable behaviors.
     - Example: "Students will be able to solve quadratic equations" rather than "students will understand quadratic equations."
2. **Relevance**
   - **Aligned with Standards:** Objectives should align with educational standards and curriculum goals.
     - Example: An objective aligned with national science standards might be "explain the water cycle and its effects on climate."
   - **Appropriate Level:** Objectives should be suitable for the students' age, grade, and skill level.
     - Example: For kindergarten, "identify basic shapes" is appropriate, while for high school geometry, "prove geometric theorems" is relevant.
3. **Measurable**
   - **Assessable:** Objectives should allow for the assessment of student progress and achievement.
     - Example: "Students will be able to write a five-paragraph essay" can be assessed through writing assignments and rubrics.

- **Quantifiable:** Where possible, objectives should include quantifiable elements.
  - Example: "Students will solve 10 math problems accurately within 15 minutes."

4. **Attainable**
   - **Realistic:** Objectives should be achievable given the students' current abilities and resources available.
     - Example: "Students will improve their reading comprehension by one grade level over the semester" is realistic if the appropriate support is provided.
5. **Time-bound**
   - **Time-specific:** Objectives should include a timeframe for completion.
     - Example: "Students will complete a science project on renewable energy sources by the end of the term."

Purpose of Educational Objectives

Educational objectives serve multiple critical purposes in the educational process, benefiting both educators and students:

1. **Provide Direction and Focus**
   - **For Educators:** Objectives help teachers plan and organize instruction, ensuring that lessons and activities are aligned with desired outcomes.
   - **For Students:** Clear objectives give students a roadmap of what they need to learn and achieve, helping them stay focused and motivated.
2. **Facilitate Assessment and Evaluation**
   - **Measuring Progress:** Objectives provide benchmarks for assessing student progress and performance. They help in designing assessments that are aligned with the intended learning outcomes.
   - **Guiding Feedback:** Educators can use objectives to give specific feedback, highlighting areas of strength and areas needing improvement.

3. **Enhance Motivation and Engagement**
   - **Setting Expectations:** Objectives make learning goals explicit, helping students understand the relevance and importance of their studies.
   - **Encouraging Achievement:** Achievable objectives can motivate students by providing a sense of accomplishment when they meet the specified goals.
4. **Ensure Consistency and Coherence**
   - **Across Curriculum:** Objectives ensure that different teachers and classes within the same grade or subject are working towards the same goals, maintaining consistency in what students are expected to learn.
   - **Vertical Alignment:** They help in creating a coherent progression of learning objectives across grade levels, ensuring that foundational skills are built upon in subsequent years.
5. **Guide Curriculum Development**
   - **Content Selection:** Objectives help in selecting appropriate content and instructional materials that support the desired learning outcomes.
   - **Instructional Strategies:** They inform the choice of teaching methods and strategies that are most effective in achieving the objectives.
6. **Support Accountability**
   - **Transparency:** Objectives make the expectations and goals of education transparent to all stakeholders, including students, parents, educators, and policymakers.
   - **Responsibility:** They hold educators accountable for delivering instruction that meets defined standards and outcomes.

Conclusion

Educational objectives are fundamental to the teaching and learning process. Their characteristics—clarity, relevance, measurability, attainability, and time-boundedness—ensure that they effectively guide instruction, assessment, and student learning. The purposes of educational objectives include providing direction, facilitating assessment, enhancing motivation, ensuring consistency, guiding curriculum development, and supporting accountability. By focusing on well-defined educational objectives, educators can create a structured and effective learning environment that promotes student success and development.

3.3 Difference between educational aims and objectives.

Difference Between Educational Aims and Objectives

Educational aims and objectives are often used interchangeably, but they serve different purposes and have distinct characteristics in the educational process. Here's a detailed explanation of their differences:

1. **Scope and Specificity**

- **Educational Aims:**
  - **Broad and General:** Aims are broad, general statements that reflect the overall goals or purposes of education. They outline the long-term vision of what education seeks to achieve.
  - **Example:** "To develop well-rounded individuals who are capable of critical thinking and lifelong learning."
- **Educational Objectives:**
  - **Specific and Detailed:** Objectives are specific, detailed statements that describe what students should know, be able to do, or value at the end of a lesson, course, or program.
  - **Example:** "Students will be able to solve quadratic equations using the quadratic formula by the end of the unit."

2. **Time Frame**

- **Educational Aims:**
  - **Long-term:** Aims are focused on long-term educational outcomes and goals that may span several years or even an entire educational career.

    - **Example:** "To prepare students to be responsible citizens and active participants in a democratic society."
- **Educational Objectives:**
    - **Short-term:** Objectives are focused on short-term learning outcomes that can be achieved within a specific timeframe, such as a lesson, unit, semester, or academic year.
    - **Example:** "Students will be able to identify and describe the main causes of World War I by the end of the week."

3. **Level of Abstraction**

- **Educational Aims:**
    - **Abstract:** Aims are more abstract and philosophical in nature. They express the values, beliefs, and overarching purposes of education.
    - **Example:** "To foster a love of learning and curiosity about the world."
- **Educational Objectives:**
    - **Concrete:** Objectives are concrete and practical. They specify measurable and observable outcomes that students are expected to achieve.
    - **Example:** "Students will be able to conduct an experiment to test the hypothesis about plant growth under different light conditions."

4. **Purpose and Function**

- **Educational Aims:**
    - **Guiding Principles:** Aims serve as guiding principles for the overall educational process. They provide a vision and direction for curriculum development, teaching strategies, and institutional goals.
    - **Example:** "To promote social equity and inclusion through education."
- **Educational Objectives:**

- **Operational Goals:** Objectives serve as operational goals that inform lesson planning, instructional methods, and assessments. They help teachers plan specific activities and measure student progress.
- **Example:** "Students will be able to write a persuasive essay with a clear thesis statement and supporting arguments."

5. Examples of Usage

- **Educational Aims:**
  - Used in mission statements, educational philosophies, and policy documents to outline the fundamental purposes and values of an educational institution or system.
  - Example: A school's mission might state, "Our aim is to nurture students to become compassionate, knowledgeable, and engaged global citizens."

- **Educational Objectives:**
  - Used in lesson plans, syllabi, and curriculum documents to detail specific learning outcomes and competencies that students are expected to achieve.
  - Example: A lesson plan might include the objective, "Students will be able to explain the process of mitosis and identify its stages."

Conclusion

In summary, educational aims and objectives differ primarily in their scope, specificity, time frame, level of abstraction, and purpose. Aims are broad, long-term goals that provide overall direction and reflect the values and philosophy of education, while objectives are specific, short-term goals that guide daily instruction and assessment. Understanding these differences helps educators design and implement effective curricula that align with both the overarching aims and the specific learning objectives of their educational programs.

3.4 Aims of education with reference to NEP-2020.

Aims of Education with Reference to NEP-2020

The National Education Policy (NEP) 2020 of India outlines a comprehensive vision for transforming the education system to meet the needs of the 21st century. The policy emphasizes several broad aims of education, which reflect both the aspirations of the nation and the individual growth of students. Here are the key aims of education as articulated in NEP-2020:

1. **Holistic Development of Learners**
    - **Focus on Comprehensive Growth:** NEP-2020 aims to develop all aspects of an individual's personality, including intellectual, social, physical, emotional, and moral growth.
    - **Example:** The policy promotes a multidisciplinary approach in higher education to ensure that students acquire a wide range of skills and knowledge across various domains.
2. **Equity and Inclusion**
    - **Access for All:** The policy emphasizes universal access to quality education for all children from pre-school to secondary level, irrespective of their socio-economic backgrounds.
    - **Example:** Special provisions for disadvantaged groups, including girls, socio-economically disadvantaged groups (SEDGs), and children with disabilities.
3. **Quality and Excellence**
    - **High Standards:** NEP-2020 aims to ensure high standards of educational outcomes at all levels.
    - **Example:** Establishment of standards for learning outcomes, teacher training, and curriculum design.
4. **Critical Thinking and Creativity**
    - **Encouraging Innovation:** The policy seeks to foster a culture of critical thinking, problem-solving, creativity, and innovation among students.

- **Example:** Emphasis on experiential learning, project-based learning, and inquiry-based learning approaches in the curriculum.

5. **Flexibility and Multidisciplinary**
   - **Personalized Learning Paths:** NEP-2020 promotes flexible curricula and varied learning paths to cater to different learning needs and interests of students.
   - **Example:** Introduction of multidisciplinary education at the higher education level, allowing students to choose subjects across disciplines.
6. **Ethical and Moral Values**
   - **Character Building:** The policy underscores the importance of inculcating ethical and moral values in students.
   - **Example:** Integration of value-based education into the curriculum to develop integrity, responsibility, empathy, and respect for others.
7. **Vocational Education and Skill Development**
   - **Career Readiness:** NEP-2020 emphasizes the importance of vocational education and skill development from an early age to enhance employability and entrepreneurial capabilities.
   - **Example:** Inclusion of vocational courses in the school curriculum and creating pathways for vocational education in higher education.
8. **Use of Technology**
   - **Digital Literacy:** The policy aims to leverage technology to improve the quality of education and make it more accessible.
   - **Example:** Promotion of digital learning platforms, online resources, and the use of technology in classrooms for better engagement and learning outcomes.
9. **Teacher Empowerment**
   - **Professional Development:** NEP-2020 recognizes the pivotal role of teachers and aims to empower them

through continuous professional development and improved working conditions.

- **Example:** Establishment of National Professional Standards for Teachers (NPST) to ensure ongoing development and career progression.

10. **Global Citizenship**

- **International Competence:** The policy encourages the development of global citizenship among students, making them aware of global issues and preparing them to be active participants in an interconnected world.
- **Example:** Incorporation of global issues such as climate change, sustainable development, and cultural diversity in the curriculum.

Conclusion

The aims of education as outlined in NEP-2020 reflect a holistic and forward-looking vision for the educational landscape in India. By focusing on holistic development, equity, quality, critical thinking, flexibility, ethical values, vocational skills, technology integration, teacher empowerment, and global citizenship, NEP-2020 aims to create an education system that is inclusive, adaptable, and capable of preparing students for the challenges and opportunities of the 21st century.

3.5 Bloom's taxonomy of educational objectives and revised taxonomy of educational objectives.

Bloom's taxonomy is a hierarchical model used for classifying learning objectives by levels of complexity and specificity. Bloom's Taxonomy was created to outline and clarify how learners acquire new knowledge and skills. Though the original intention of the taxonomy was to serve as an assessment tool, Bloom's taxonomy is effective in helping instructors identify clear learning objectives as well as create purposeful learning activities and instructional materials.

Bloom's taxonomy emerged from a 1948 meeting of university educators – chaired by Benjamin Bloom – who brainstormed a theoretical model of learning that identified educational objectives to aid in the creation of testing items. The committee later expanded its initial framework to three learning domains:

- Cognitive: knowledge or thinking
- Affective: growth in feelings or emotional areas (attitude or self)
- Psychomotor: manual or physical skills

Cognitive Domain

The cognitive domain went through numerous revisions before a finalized version was published (Bloom 1956).

The cognitive domain has been the primary focus in education and has become shorthand for Bloom's Taxonomy as a result. The cognitive domain is made up of six levels of objectives. These levels are organized by hierarchy, moving from foundational skills to higher-order thinking skills.

In 2001 Anderson and Krathwohl revised Bloom's levels from nouns to verbs, and this is the version of the taxonomy used today.

- Remember: retrieve relevant knowledge from memory.
- Understand: determine the meaning of instructional messages.
- Apply: use a procedure in a given situation.
- Analyze: break materials into components and determine how they work together.
- Evaluate: make judgments based on criteria and standards.
- Create: create a new or original work.

Bloom's Taxonomy of Educational Objectives and its Revised Taxonomy are hierarchical models used to classify educational learning objectives into levels of complexity and specificity. Here's an in-depth look at both:

Affective Domain

The affective domain was first published in 1964 (Krathwohl et al, 1964). The affective domain outlines skills and behaviors that correspond to attitudes and values and as the learner progresses through the levels of the affective domain, they become self-reliant and internally motivated. Learning objectives aligned to the affective domain tend to be the hardest to articulate initially and often appear difficult to assess at first glance. However, affective outcomes often represent the outcomes most closely related to deeper thinking and lifelong learning.

The affective domain contains five levels, from lowest to highest:

- Receiving: Willing to listen and receive knowledge.
- Responding: Actively participates and engages in knowledge transfer.
- Valuing: Finds value and worth in one's learning with motivation to continue.
- Organizing: Integrates and compares values, resolves conflict between these values, and orders them according to priorities.
- Characterizing: Creates a value system that controls behavior. The behavior is pervasive, consistent, predictable, and characteristic of the learner.

Psychomotor Domain

Bloom and his colleagues did not create subcategories for skills in the psychomotor domain, but other educators did (Simpson 1966, 1972; Dave, 1970; Harrow, 1972). The psychomotor domain includes physical movement, coordination, and motor skills. Development of these skills requires practice and is measured in terms of speed, precision, distance, procedures, or technical execution. For the purpose of this teaching guide, we will explore Simpson's version of the psychomotor domain, which has the following seven levels:

- **Perception**: Use sensory cues to guide actions or movements.
- **Set**: Demonstrates a readiness (physically, mentally, emotionally, and spiritually) to take action to perform the task or objective. (NOTE: This level of the Psychomotor domain is closely related to the "Responding to phenomena" level of the Affective domain).

- **Guided response**: Knows steps required to complete the task or objective and learns through trial and error by practicing.
- **Mechanism**: Performs task or objective in a somewhat confident, proficient, and habitual manner.
- **Complex overt response**: Performs task or objective in a confident, proficient, and habitual manner. Expert level, high proficiency and performs with accuracy.
- **Adaptation**: Performs task or objective and can modify actions to account for new or problematic situations.
- **Origination**: Create new procedures and solutions to approach various situations.

Original Bloom's Taxonomy (1956)

Developed by Benjamin Bloom and his colleagues, the original taxonomy categorizes cognitive skills into six hierarchical levels, from basic recall to complex evaluation:

1. **Knowledge**: Recall of facts and basic concepts.
    - **Example**: Memorizing historical dates, definitions, or formulas.
2. **Comprehension**: Understanding information and grasping meaning.
    - **Example**: Explaining the main idea of a text or summarizing a concept in one's own words.
3. **Application**: Using knowledge in new and concrete situations.
    - **Example**: Applying a mathematical formula to solve a real-world problem.
4. **Analysis**: Breaking information into parts to explore understandings and relationships.
    - **Example**: Comparing and contrasting different theories or examining arguments in an essay.

5. **Synthesis**: Compiling information in a different way by combining elements to form a new pattern or proposing alternative solutions.
    - **Example**: Writing a research paper or developing a new business plan.
6. **Evaluation**: Making judgments based on criteria and standards.
    - **Example**: Critiquing a work of art or assessing the validity of a study.

Revised Bloom's Taxonomy (2001)

In 2001, a group led by Lorin Anderson (a former student of Bloom) and David Krathwohl updated the taxonomy to reflect a more active form of thinking. The revision involves changes in terminology and structure:

1. **Remembering**: Retrieving, recognizing, and recalling relevant knowledge.
    - **Example**: Listing the stages of cell division.
2. **Understanding**: Constructing meaning from oral, written, and graphic messages.
    - **Example**: Interpreting the significance of a graph or summarizing a chapter of a book.
3. **Applying**: Carrying out or using a procedure in a given situation.
    - **Example**: Using knowledge of physics to calculate the trajectory of a projectile.
4. **Analyzing**: Breaking material into constituent parts and detecting how the parts relate to one another and to an overall structure or purpose.
    - **Example**: Analyzing the themes and techniques used in a piece of literature.
5. **Evaluating**: Making judgments based on criteria and standards through checking and critiquing.
    - **Example**: Evaluating the credibility of sources in an academic paper.

6. **Creating**: Putting elements together to form a coherent or functional whole; reorganizing elements into a new pattern or structure.
    - **Example**: Designing an experiment to test a hypothesis or writing a novel.

Comparison of the Two Taxonomies

Original Taxonomy:

1. Knowledge
2. Comprehension
3. Application
4. Analysis
5. Synthesis
6. Evaluation

Revised Taxonomy:

1. Remembering
2. Understanding
3. Applying
4. Analyzing
5. Evaluating
6. **Creating**

Key Changes and Implications

- **Terminology**: The revised taxonomy uses verbs (e.g., "Remembering" instead of "Knowledge") to emphasize the active nature of thinking and learning.
- **Structure**: "Synthesis" was renamed "Creating" and moved to the highest level, reflecting a focus on generating new ideas and products.
- **Process Dimensions**: The revised taxonomy introduces a dual-dimensional framework, combining the cognitive process dimension (the six categories above) with a knowledge dimension (factual, conceptual, procedural, and metacognitive knowledge).

Educational Implications:

Application in Education

- **Curriculum Design**

  Educators use Bloom's Taxonomy to design curricula that foster a range of cognitive skills. By including objectives at all levels of the taxonomy, teachers can ensure that students are not only recalling information but also understanding, applying, analyzing, synthesizing, and evaluating it.

- **Lesson Planning**

  Teachers use the taxonomy to plan lessons that encourage higher-order thinking. For example, a lesson on ecosystems might begin with students recalling facts about different biomes (Knowledge), explaining the food chain (Comprehension), applying their knowledge by classifying animals into different biomes (Application), analyzing the impact of human activities on ecosystems (Analysis), creating a model of an ecosystem (Synthesis), and evaluating the effectiveness of conservation strategies (Evaluation).

- **Assessment Design**

  Assessments can be structured to evaluate different levels of cognitive ability. Multiple-choice questions might test knowledge and comprehension, while essays and projects might assess application, analysis, synthesis, and evaluation.

- **Instructional Strategies**

  Teachers can employ a variety of instructional strategies to target different levels of the taxonomy. For example, direct instruction and rote memorization might be used for knowledge and comprehension, while project-based learning and Socratic questioning might be used for analysis and evaluation.

Conclusion

Both the original and revised Bloom's Taxonomies provide valuable frameworks for educators. The revised taxonomy, with its emphasis on active verbs and reordering of the highest cognitive processes, aligns more closely with modern educational goals, promoting a deeper, more comprehensive approach to teaching and learning.

3.6 Classification of Educational Objectives according to Indian classrooms.

The classification of educational objectives in Indian classrooms can be effectively understood through the framework proposed by educational psychologist Benjamin Bloom, known as Bloom's Taxonomy. This taxonomy is often adapted to suit different educational contexts, including those in India. Here's an overview of how Bloom's Taxonomy can be applied to Indian classrooms:

Bloom's Taxonomy Overview

Bloom's Taxonomy categorizes educational objectives into three domains: Cognitive, Affective, and Psychomotor. Each domain has hierarchical levels that represent increasing complexity and mastery.

1. Cognitive Domain (Knowledge-Based)

This domain focuses on intellectual skills and knowledge acquisition. The levels in this domain are:

1. **Remembering:** Recalling facts and basic concepts (e.g., memorizing multiplication tables, historical dates).
2. **Understanding:** Explaining ideas or concepts (e.g., summarizing a story, explaining a scientific principle).
3. **Applying:** Using information in new situations (e.g., solving math problems using learned formulas)
4. **Analyzing:** Breaking information into parts to understand it better (e.g., comparing different political systems, identifying themes in a novel).
5. **Evaluating:** Justifying a decision or course of action (e.g., critiquing an essay, assessing the effectiveness of a scientific experiment).
6. **Creating:** Producing new or original work (e.g., writing a poem, designing an experiment).

2. Affective Domain (Attitude-Based) This domain addresses emotions, attitudes, and values. The levels are:

1. **Receiving:** Being aware of or attending to something in the environment (e.g., listening to a lecture, watching a demonstration).
2. **Responding:** Actively participating or reacting to the environment (e.g., participating in a discussion, answering questions).
3. **Valuing:** Recognizing the worth of something and expressing preferences (e.g., showing appreciation for cultural diversity).
4. **Organizing:** Integrating different values and resolving conflicts between them (e.g., balancing schoolwork and extracurricular activities).
5. **Characterizing:** Acting consistently according to a set of values (e.g., demonstrating academic integrity, showing empathy).

3. Psychomotor Domain (Skills-Based): This domain involves physical movement, coordination, and the use of motor skills. The levels are:

1. **Perception:** Using sensory cues to guide motor activity (e.g., recognizing cues in a dance routine).
2. **Set:** Readiness to act (e.g., being prepared to participate in physical education activities).
3. **Guided Response:** Performing under guidance, often with trial and error (e.g., practicing handwriting, following a recipe).
4. **Mechanism:** Gaining proficiency in performing tasks (e.g., typing with accuracy, playing a musical instrument).
5. **Complex Overt Response:** Performing complex movements smoothly (e.g., executing a complex gymnastic routine).
6. **Adaptation:** Modifying movements to suit different situations (e.g., adapting a dance to a new rhythm).
7. **Origination:** Creating new movement patterns (e.g., choreographing a dance).

Application in Indian Classrooms: Indian classrooms, characterized by diversity in language, culture, and socio-economic backgrounds, often adapt Bloom's Taxonomy to meet specific educational needs. Here's how it can be applied:

- **Primary Education:** Emphasis on the foundational levels of the cognitive domain (Remembering, Understanding, Applying) to build basic literacy and numeracy skills.
- **Secondary Education:** Focus on higher-order thinking skills (Analyzing, Evaluating, Creating) to prepare students for board exams and higher education.
- **Affective Objectives:** Integration of values education, moral science, and social studies to instill cultural values, empathy, and civic responsibility.
- **Skill Development:** Emphasis on the psychomotor domain in vocational training, physical education, and co-curricular activities to ensure holistic development.

Examples of Implementation.

- **Science Classes:** Conducting experiments (Applying, Analyzing), writing lab reports (Creating, Evaluating).
- **Language Classes:** Reading comprehension (Understanding), writing essays (Creating), participating in debates (Evaluating).
- **Social Studies:** Discussing historical events (Remembering, Understanding), analyzing current events (Analyzing), conducting projects on social issues (Creating).

By tailoring Bloom's Taxonomy to the context of Indian classrooms, educators can create a structured and comprehensive approach to learning that addresses the cognitive, affective, and psychomotor needs of students.

UNIT 4: SKILL BASED TEACHING

Teaching Skills Every professional demand certain specific skill and competency in their professional area for producing maximum output within optimum cost and time. Teaching profession is a process of social engineering. Hence it should be taken place effectively and efficiently. A skilled teacher can make wonders in their profession and can influence the learning process as well as the learning outcome of the students and help them to achieve their life goals. Teaching skills are essential for effective teaching. Teaching skill can be defined as a set of interrelated expressive behaviour of the teacher (verbal and nonverbal) which can be observable, explainable, assessable, demonstrable and refinable through perfect practices. N.L.

Gage (1968) defined "Teaching skills are specific instructional activities and procedures that a teacher may use in his classroom. These are related to the various stages of teaching or in the continuous flow of the teacher's performance."

4.1 Phases of teaching: pre-active phase, interactive phase, post-active phase.

Phases and Variables of Teaching

Introduction

Teaching is an important part of the process of education. Its special function is to impart knowledge, develop understanding and skills. Teaching is associated with 7 R's. teaching is an integral part of the process of education. It is a system of actions intended to induce learning. In teaching, an interaction occurs between the teachers and the students, by which the students are diverted towards their goal.

Teaching can be considered as the art of assisting another to learn by providing the information and appropriate situations, conditions or activities. It is a process by which one person helps other in the achievement of knowledge, skill and aptitudes.

Anatomy/Structure/Variables of Teaching-

Teaching consists of three variables, which operate in the phases of teaching and determines the nature and format of learning conditions or situations. They are: –

i. Independent variables (The Teacher)
ii. Intervening variables (Learning experience)
iii. Dependent Variables (The Student)

Teacher as an Independent Variable-

The teacher plays the role of independent variables. Students are dependent on him in the teaching process. The teacher does the planning, organizing, leading and controlling of teaching for bringing about behavioral change in the students. He is free to perform various activities for providing learning experience to students.

Content and methodology of presentation as intervening variables: -

The intervening variables lead to interaction between the teacher and the students. The content determines the mode of presentation- telling, showing and doing etc.

Students as Dependent Variable

The students are required to act according to the planning and organization of the teacher. Teaching activities of the teacher influence the learning of the students.

Phases of Teaching

Teaching is a complex task. For performing this task, a systematic planning is needed. Teaching is to be considered in terms of various steps and the different steps constituting the process are called the phases of teaching. If we want to obtain a complete description of the teaching activities, we must consider what the teacher does before, during and after his regular teaching in the class.

We can divide the teaching act into three phases as shown below: –

a. Pre-active Phase or the Planning Phase
b. Inter-active Phase or the Implementation Phase
c. Post-active Phase or Evaluation Phase.

A. PRE-ACTIVE PHASE OF TEACHING

In the pre-active phase of teaching, the planning of teaching is carried over. This phase includes all those activities which a teacher performs before classroom teaching or before entering into the classroom.

Pre-active consists essentially of the planning of a lesson. The planning of lesson needs to be seen in broader terms, not merely the designing of a lesson plan. Planning includes identifying the objectives to be achieved in terms of students learning, the strategies and methods to be adopted, use of teaching learning aids and so on.

Planning is done for taking decision about the following aspects: -

i. Selection of the content to be taught.

ii. Organization of the content.

iii. Justification of the principles and maxims of teaching to be used.

iv. Selection of the appropriate methods of teaching.

v. Decision about the preparation and usage of evaluation tools.

Suggested activities in the Pre-active Phase: -

a. **Determining goals or objectives**: - First of all, the teacher determines the teaching objectives which are then defined in terms of expected behavioral change. Thus, he ascertains the teaching objectives and what changes he expects in the students by achieving these objectives. These objectives are determined according to the psychology of the pupils and needs of the school and society.

b. **Selection of the content to be taught:** - After fixing the teaching objectives, the teacher makes decision about that content which is to be presented before the pupils and as a result he wants to bring the changes in their behavior. This decision is taken by the teacher by considering the following points: -

i. Level, needs and importance of the curriculum proposed by the teacher for the students.
ii. The expected terminal behavior of the students.
iii. Level and mode of motivation be used for the students.
iv. Selection of appropriate instrument and methods the teacher should use to evaluate the knowledge related to the content.

c. **Sequencing the elements of content for presentation**: - After making selections regarding the contents to be presented to the students, the teacher arranges the elements of content in a logical and psychological manner, so that these arrangements of content may assist in transfer of learning.
d. **Selection about the instructional methodology**: - After sequencing the contents, the teacher makes decision regarding the proper methods and strategies by keeping in view the contents, entering behavior and the level of the students.
e. **How and when of teaching strategies**: - Decision making regarding the teaching methods and strategies for presenting the sequenced contents to the students is not sufficient. So, the teacher should also decide how and when he will make use of the previously selected method and strategy during the classroom teaching.

B. INTERACTIVE PHASE OF TEACHING

The second phase includes the execution of the plan, where learning experiences are provided to students through suitable modes.

An instruction is a complex process by which learners are provided with a deliberately designed environment to interact with, keeping in focus pre-specified objectives of bringing about specific desirable changes whether instruction goes in a classroom, laboratory, outdoors or library, this environment is specially designed by a teacher so that students interact with certain specific environmental stimuli, like natural components (outdoor), information from books, certain equipment (laboratory) etc. Learning is directed in pre-determined directions to achieve certain pre-specific goals. This does not, however, mean that, in the pre-determined environment no learning other than what a teacher ha decided upon as instructional objectives does not take place. The variety of experiences that students go through with a teacher, among themselves provide learning opportunities.

All those activities which are performed by a teacher after entering in a class are clubbed under inter-active phase of teaching. Generally, these activities are concerned with the presentation and activities are concerned with the presentation and delivery of the content in a class. The teacher provides pupil verbal stimulation of various kinds, makes explanations, ask questions, listen to the student's response and provide guidance. The following are the activities suggested for the inclusion in the inter-active phase: -

i. **Sizing-up the class**: – As the teacher enters the classroom, first of all he/she perceives the size of the class. He/she throws his/her eyes on all the pupils of the class in a few moments. He comes to know the pupils who can help him/her in his/her teaching and the pupil who can create a problem for him as a result of this perception. In the same way, the students can feel the personality of the teacher. Hence, at this stage the teacher should look like a teacher. He/she should exhibit of course in a veiled manner. In a nutshell, the teacher should appear as an efficient and impressive personality.

ii. **Knowledge of learners: –** After having a feeling of class-size, the teacher makes efforts to know how much the new comers or pupils have previous knowledge. The teacher tries to know the abilities, interests and attitudes and academic background of learners.

The teacher starts teaching activities after diagnosing, by questioning regarding action and reaction. Two types of activities are involved here in the teaching –

a. Initiation

b. Response

Both these activities are known as verbal interaction. Both these activities occur between the teacher and the students. In other words, when a teacher performs some activities, the student reacts or when students perform some activities, the teacher reacts. This way the inter-action in the teaching take place.

The teacher performs the following activities in order to analyze the nature of verbal and non verbal inter-action of teaching activities: -

i. Selection and presentation of stimuli
ii. Feedback and reinforcement
iii. Deployment of strategies.

Selection and presentation of stimuli

The teacher should select the appropriate stimulus as soon as the situation arises and an effect should be made to control the undesired activities to create the situation and for desired activities.

Feedback and reinforcement

Feedback or reinforcement is that condition which increases the possibility for accepting a particular response in future. These conditions may be of two types: –

a. Positive reinforcement
b. Negative Reinforcement

Reinforcement is used for three purposes. These are: –

a. For strengthening the response
b. For changing the response
c. For modifying or correcting the response.

Development of strategies

The teaching activities are directly related to the learning conditions. Therefore, at the time of interaction, the teacher produces such activities and conditions by the reinforcement strategies which effect the activities of the pupil.

Major operations of inter-active phase are –

a. Perception
b. Diagnosis
c. Response

Perception: – Interaction process demands an appropriate perception on the part of teacher as well as the students. When a teacher enters the class, his first activity is concerned with a perception of the classroom climate. He tries to weigh himself, his abilities for teaching against the class group. Similarly, students also try to have perception of the abilities, behavior and personality characteristics of the teacher.

Diagnosis: – A teacher tries to access the achievement level of his students with regards to their abilities, interest and aptitude. The teacher can ask several questions to know how far students know about the topic.

Reaction/Response: - Under this stage, teacher observes the students that how they respond to the teacher's question. The student has to learn the proper way of reacting and responding to the various stimuli and teaching techniques presented to it. This phase is responsible for establishing appropriate verbal and non-verbal classroom interaction between teacher and pupils.

C. POST-ACTIVE PHASE OF TEACHING-

Post-active phase is the one that involves teacher's activities such as analyzing evaluation results to determine student's learning, especially their problems in understanding specific areas, to reflect on the teaching by self, and to decide on the necessary change to be brought into the system in the next instructional period.

The post-active phase concerns with the evaluation activities. This can be done in number of ways including tests or quizzes or by observing student's reaction of question, comments, structures and instructed situations.

In this phase, as the teaching task sums up, the teacher asks questions to the pupils, verbally or in written form, to measure the behavior of the pupils so that their achievements may be evaluated correctly.

The following activities are suggested in the post-active phase of teaching—

a. Defining the exact dimensions of the changes caused by teaching.

b. Selecting appropriate testing devices and techniques.

c. Changing the strategies in terms of evidences gathered.

Defining the exact dimensions of the changes caused by teaching: At the end of teaching, the teacher defines the exact dimensions of changes in the behavior as a result of teaching. This is termed as criterion behavior. For this, the teacher compares the actual behavioral changes in the students with their expected behavioral changes. If he observes the desired behavioral changes in the maximum numbers of pupils, he concludes that his teaching strategies and tactics worked effectively with the help of which teaching objectives have been achieved.

Selecting appropriate testing devices and techniques: -

The teacher selects those testing devices and techniques to compare the actual behavioral change with the desired behavioral change which are reliable and valid and which can evaluate the cognitive and non-cognitive aspects of the pupils. Therefore, criterion tests are more preferred than the performed tests.

Changing the strategies in terms of evidences gathered: -

While by using the reliable and valid testing devices, the teacher gets the knowledge regarding the performances of pupils and attainment of objectives on one hand, and on the other hand, he also gets clarity regarding his instruction, teaching strategies and tactics. He also comes to know about the required modification in the teaching strategies and situation along with the drawbacks of his teaching in order to achieve the teaching objectives. In this way, through evaluation, the teaching activities are diagnosed and this can be made effective by necessary modification and change in them.

4.2 Levels of teaching: memory, understanding and reflective.

LEVELS OF TEACHING

Teaching is a purposive activity; the purpose is to bring about desirable changes in the learner through learning. Three levels of teaching are:

I- Memory Level – Thoughtless
II- Understanding Level – Thoughtful
III-Reflective Level – Upper Thoughtful

I-Memory Level of Teaching: The objective of teaching at this level is just to impart information to students. The learner is required to memorize the subject matter and get the information stored in long term memory. Herbart is considered the exponent of memory level of teaching. The learner has to learn the material, retain the meaningful material and reproduce that when asked for. Elements of Memory Level of Teaching:

Elements of Memory Level of Teaching:

1. Objective: The Objective of the Memory Level of teaching is Just to impart information or knowledge to the learner. This knowledge or information is factual in nature, which is acquired through a mechanical process (i.e. memorization or rote learning)

2. Aims of Memory Level of Teaching:

a. To get factual information
b. To train memory faculty
c. To retrain the learning material in-memory storage
d. To reproduce and recognize the learned information when required Memory Level covers only the knowledge-based objective of Bloom's taxonomy where the students learn to identify, recall or remember the objects, events, ideas, and concepts and retain them in memory.

3. Nature of Subject Matter in Memory Level

a. Subject matter should be structured and well organized and of simple nature that can be acquired through rote learning and can be retained and recalled.
b. Subject matter included information about simple concepts, terms, and elements related to different things of the world around.

4. Methods Used by the teacher in-memory level of teaching: Teacher dominated methods are used- like drill, review, and revision and asking questions. Drill means repetition or practice for the purpose of attaining proficiency in memorizing the material. Review and Revision is revising the elements to related them with new experience and to form a new association for the development of new skills or learning to solve new problems Asking question is to examine whether or not the knowledge level objectives of teaching have been achieved.

5. **Role of The Teacher in Memory Level of Teaching**:
   a. Dominating, active and authoritarian role
   b. He is the authority to instruct, deliver, direct, control and evaluate the performances
   c. Takes initiatives, present the subject matter, directs the learner to do the activity in the desired manner, plan exercises
   d. Right from the selection of the subject matter to its evaluation, the key process of teaching-learning remains with the teacher.
6. **Role of Learner in Memory Level of Teaching**: There is a Passive role of the learner in the memory level. Passive listener desired to do as directed by the teacher Instructional material delivered by the teacher and the learner has to memorize it in a mechanical manner. Little understanding is applied by the learner.
7. **Teaching Equipment used by the teacher in Memory level of teaching**: Teaching aids like visual, audio and audiovisual aids, e.g. Models, charts, maps, pictures, TV, Radio, Computer, film strips, etc. should be sued to develop curiosity among the students.
8. **Nature of motivation which is required in memory level**: When students learn something naturally, we call it intrinsic motivation When learning is caused by external forces, we call it extrinsic motivation. In the memory level of teaching the nature of motivation is extrinsic.

9. Evaluation System:

a) Oral and written tests are used to test the memory of the students

b) In evaluation, written test, short type test, recall type, recognition type, multiple-choice, alternative type, and matching type the test is employed

Merits/ Advantages and Importance of Memory Level of Teaching:

a) Useful for young children

b) Useful for the acquisition of facts, information of models and structure

c) Help children learn a new concept

d) Useful for slow learners

e) The basis for understanding and reflective level of teaching.

Demerits / Disadvantages of Memory Level of Teaching:

a) Not suitable for higher classes

b) Use of rote memory

c) Dominance of teacher

d) Little interaction in the classroom

e) No room for initiation and self-learning for the students

f) Not intrinsic motivation

g) Problem of classroom management

h) Loss of retention and recall

Suggestions for Memory Level Teaching:

a) Teaching material should be meaningful and purposeful

b) Adequate and appropriate teaching aids

c) Subject matter should be integrated and well-sequenced

d) Continuous evaluation

e) More drill work

f) Motivation

g) Whole to the part method should be used

h) Repetition

i) Practice and exercise

II-Understanding Level of Teaching:

Understanding implies to know the meanings of things and concepts, to grasp ideas, to interpret some relationship, to comprehend the facts and to infer one thing from some other. At this level, the learners and required to comprehend factual information, to know the meaning of different concepts and their relationships and to apply facts, concepts, and principles. It is supported by the Herbartian Theory of apperception, which states that this level of teaching seeks the learner to acquaint himself with the relationship between the facts and principles. Here the mental development of the learner is at a higher level than memory level. His cognitive abilities are well developed now; he can think, reason out, imagine, can present things logically; can analyze and synthesize, and can evaluate the relationship between the principles and facts. Development of cognitive abilities of the learner is at the operational stage as stated by Jean Piaget. Learner at this stage needs to comprehend a large number of concepts, elements, facts, principles; to know the relationship between facts and principles, to make a generalization and to draw interference there from.

Steps of Herbartian Theory of Apperception:

a) Preparation and Introduction
b) Presentation
c) Comparison, Association, and Abstraction
d) Generalization
e) Application
f) Evaluation

Elements of the Understanding level of Teaching:

1. **Aims and Objectives: According to Bloom's Taxonomy of Educational Objectives (1956): Comprehension Objectives**: Comprised of: Translation. Interpretations and extrapolation **Application Objective:** Efficiency to apply to comprehend knowledge in various similar and different situations and settings.

According to Bloom's revised Taxonomy:

Understanding Objectives: It pertains to the Understanding of instructional messages (Maybe oral, written or graphical, etc.), By means of Interpretation, exemplifying, classifying, summarizing, inferring, comparing and explaining, etc.

Application Objective: Application objectives include the use of the proper procedure for Executing Implementing; the use of generalized rule or principle in practical life situations. The student acquaints themselves with the ideas for facts with full understanding and their application.

2. **Nature of Subject matter:**
   Nature of subject matter is wide, larger in number and quality.
3. **Methods used**: Lecture method, Lecture demonstration method, Discussion method Inductive and deductive method, Exemplification and explanation.
4. **Classroom Climate:** The classroom climate is more lively and encouraging the problem of discipline is also less
5. **Nature of Motivation:**
   Students start learning at this level for two reasons, they are asked by the teacher to learn, their internal forces insist upon them to learn.
6. **Teaching Equipment:** Different charts, models, flashcards, pictures, TV and many more electronic devices are used as teaching equipment.
7. **Evaluation:** The teacher has to evaluate the ability to comprehend, grasp, synthesize, discriminate and generalize; and the insight to apply the generalized principles further so, the tests and tools should be properly planned and devised. Besides asking questions for oral testing, written testing should be conducted.
8. **Role of the teacher**: The teacher is a prominent figure. Not so dominating and authoritarian
9. **Role of the learner:** The role of the learner in understating the level of teaching is not so passive. He may put questions to clarify his doubts.

Merits/ advantages and importance of understating the level of teaching:

1. Effective learning 2. Development of different cognition abilities 3. Sets stages for entering into the reflective level of teaching 4. Effective classroom interaction.

Demerits or disadvantages of Understanding Level of Teaching: 1. It ignores higher cognitive abilities 2. Less emphasis on intrinsic motivation 3. No individualized learning 4. Teacher centered

Suggestions for Understanding Level of teaching:

1. There should be effective classroom interaction 2. Organized subject matter 3. Meaningfulness for the subject –matter 4. An effective method of teaching 5. Use of teaching aids 6. Proper classroom environment

III-Reflective Level of Teaching: This Level of teaching is the highest level of teaching-learning activity. It is the stage of learning when students do not merely repeat and revise or answer the questions as asked for; nor do they only understand, learn, interrelate or interpret the concepts but also, they ponder upon, contemplate and pay serious thoughtful consideration to the presented contents.

Definition: Morris L. Bigge defines reflection as, "careful, critical examination of an idea or supposed article of knowledge in the light of testing evidence which supports it and the further conclusions towards which it points. Reflective level teaching does not depend upon the memorization, understanding of concepts and their application only; it demands the use of higher mental processes such as reasoning, thinking, analyzing concepts, imagination, ideas and thoughts; and other bodies of knowledge critically, finding out the facts.

Reflective level teaching-learning comprises the highest level of learning by the learner to develop new insight to solve problems, to explore the field of knowledge, to discover, to test and retest the achieved facts, to understand and present generalizations in the light of the new evidence.

Elements of Reflective Level of Teaching:

1. Objectives: To develop insight into the learner to solve problems. To develop rational and critical thinking in the students. To develop the ability of independent thinking and decision making in the students.

2. Nature of Subject Matter: This level of teaching the subject matter is mainly unstructured and open-ended. It is concerned with the problem rather than the subject.

3. Teaching Learning Process: The process of teaching and learning at this level is dynamic and unique. The students are provided with problematic situations and they need to follow certain procedures to solve the problems independently.

4. Methods Used:

1. Problem-solving method
2. Investigating projects
3. Heuristic method
4. Experimental method
5. Inquiry oriented method
6. Analytic method

5. Nature of Motivation: The Nature of motivation is intrinsic because of all learning activities depend upon the felt need of the learner.

6. Evaluation System: The Evaluation System at the reflective level of teaching should test the higher-order cognitive abilities like reasoning, creativity, original thinking, problem-solving, critical thinking, etc.

7. Role of the teacher: The role of the teacher is not so dominating and authoritarian. He is responsible for the creation and maintenance of the democratic, dynamic atmosphere where the teaching learning activities can be carried out smoothly.

Merits or Advantages of Reflective Level of Teaching:

1. It is the most thoughtful mode of operation.
2. Learner-centered approach
3. Development of problem-solving ability
4. Useful for gifted children.
5. Provides maximum flexibility
6. Self-motivation

7. Development of creativity

Demerits of Reflective Level of Teaching:

1. It is not suitable for lower classes
2. It is a time-consuming process.
3. This level of teaching is not suitable for the Indian classroom.
4. It is not applicable for dull students.
5. There is an excess burden to the teacher.

Suggestions for the reflective level of teaching:

1. The proper atmosphere should be provided.
2. Creating problematic situations.
3. Proper direction
4. Proper evaluation
5. Encourage independent learning

4.3 Principles and maxims of teaching.

Every profession needs proven facts and universal facts to understand and work. As every profession has its facts based on the experiences of people practicing that particular profession, so is the teaching profession. Maxims of teaching are the universally found facts by teachers on the basis of their experience. It is important for every profession to have some rules, ethics, code, and other boundaries to practice that profession with utter fairness and trust.

Maxims of Teaching: –

The maxims of teaching energize both the teacher and the taught and make them active and co-operative. Maxims of teaching also help in arousing interest and motivating students. Keeping in view the importance of maxims in the teaching learning process, some of the important maxims of teaching are discussed below: -

Maxims of Teaching

Maxims are short statements like a dictum that are treated as general rule of conduct

- From Known to Unknown
- From Simple to Complex
- From Concrete to Abstract
- From Particular to General
- From Whole to Part
- From Psychological to Logical
- From Induction to Deduction
- From Empirical to Rational
- From Analysis to Synthesis

Maxims of Teaching-

a. **Proceed from known to unknown**: - The most natural and simple way of teaching a lesson is to proceed from something that the pupils already know to those facts which they do not know. Previous knowledge serves as a solid foundation in the acquisition of new knowledge. For making teaching effective and fruitful, a teacher should proceed step by step to connect new knowledge with old knowledge.

b. **Proceed form simple to complex**: – To develop a sense of satisfaction in students, simple and easy lessons should be taught first to be followed by complex and difficult one. The word easy to difficult or complex should be viewed from child's standpoint not from adults. In teaching, the teacher should begin with the most striking and prominent features of a topic and then proceed to the detail.

c. **Proceed from easy to difficult**: - Subject matter should be graded in such a way so that children can climb the ladder of subject or lesson with ease and little difficulty. This is possible if easy lessons precede the difficult ones. In determining the level of difficulty, children's psychological set up should be taken into consideration.

d. **Proceed from concrete to abstract**: – Children can learn things easily when they can see and handle them. The idea of two plus two is equal to four (2+2=4) is an abstract idea. If the same things are done by allowing children to count two sticks with another two sticks, the idea of four will easily come to their mind. The process of concretization makes learning interesting and lively. A lesson of geography can be made interesting with the help of maps, charts, globes, models, pictures of mountains, river, etc.

e. Proceed from particular to general: - The particular instances are simple, definite and concrete whereas generalizations are likely to be complex and abstract. The process of learning can only become complete if children can proceed from particular and finish with the general rules or definitions. The rules of arithmetic, of grammar, of physical geography and almost of all sciences are based on this principle of proceeding from particular instances to general rules. For example- in teaching algebra, formulae should be derived from particular cases and then applied to solve more problems. So to ensure better understanding both inductive and deductive methods should be applied.

f. Proceed from indefinite to definite: – In the early stages, children's ideas and knowledges are indefinite and vague. The objective of teaching is to make these indefinite ideas definite, clear, precise, coherent and systematic. This can be done by making children interested in lessons, developing their power of observation and encouraging them to take active part in the process of learning. Every word and idea presented to the child should be clear. For this purpose, the use of pictures, actual objects, diagrams and other devices should be frequently made.

g. Proceed from empirical to rational: - It is generally argued that first of all a child acquires knowledge from the experience of his day-to-day life and after that they feels the rational bases. So, understanding of rational knowledge is not possible at early stage because children cannot comprehend abstract concepts. Rational knowledge is possible only when children attain some level of mental maturity. Empirical knowledge serves at the base for mental development which in turn leads to rational knowledge.

h. **Proceed from psychological to logical**: – Logical approach is concerned with the arrangement of the subject matter whereas, psychological approach looks at the child's interests, needs, mental make and reactions. But for effective teaching subject matter should be arranged in accordance with the mental development of the children. The approach should be based on children's tendencies, interests, aptitudes, attitudes and reactions. For example- while teaching arithmetic, simple problems should come after the students have mastered counting up to ten or so. Thus, the process of teaching should proceed along psychological lines. Though the aim of education is to make mind more logical and to train the reasoning power, yet the initial approach of teaching should be psychological rather than logical.

i. **Proceed from whole to part**: – Whole is more meaningful to the child than the parts of the whole. Researchers have proved that the whole approach is better than the part approach. While putting emphasis on whole, one important point to be noted here is that the whole should be integrated in terms of child's understanding. Moreover, the whole for a slow reader is smaller than the whole for a fast reader. Thus, it is essential to form meaningful whole.

j. **Proceed from analysis to synthesis**: – Analysis means breaking a problem into convenient parts, while synthesis means grouping of these parts into a complete whole. For example- in language study, children begin with sentences expressing simple idea. These sentences are analyzed into subject, verb and object. This process helps the child to have knowledge about the formation of sentence. But fuller understanding of the meaning of the sentence comes only when words are again arranged so as to make a sentence. Thus, analysis must be followed by synthesis otherwise analysis is fruitless.

4.4 Skill based teaching.

The world is changing fast, and so are the skills you need to thrive in it. You may have noticed that the education system you grew up with is not keeping up with the pace of innovation and disruption. It is still focused on memorizing facts and theories rather than developing practical skills and competencies that you can apply in real-life situations. That's why skill-based education is the way to go. It is a learning approach that helps you master the skills that matter in the 21st century.

What is skill-based education?

Skill-based education is a type of education that focuses on developing specific skills and competencies that are useful and applicable in real-world situations. Unlike traditional education, which mainly emphasizes acquiring theoretical knowledge and information, skill-based education aims to equip learners with practical abilities and attitudes that can help them solve problems, create opportunities, and achieve their goals.

Skill-based education can cover a wide range of domains, such as technical skills, digital skills, communication skills, interpersonal skills, leadership skills, entrepreneurial skills, etc. Skill-based education can also be tailored to the needs and interests of different learners, such as students, workers, professionals, entrepreneurs, etc.

Benefits of skill-based education.

For learners, skill-based education can help them:

- Develop their confidence, creativity, critical thinking, problem-solving, communication, teamwork, and leadership skills.
- Acquire the technical and vocational skills that are in high demand in various sectors and industries.
- Improve their employability, career prospects, income potential, and lifelong learning opportunities.

For teachers, skill-based education can help them:

- Design more engaging, interactive, and personalized learning experiences for their students.

- Use more diverse and innovative teaching methods and tools, such as online platforms, multimedia resources, gamification, etc.
- Collaborate more effectively with other teachers, employers, and experts to enrich their professional development and knowledge.

Skill-based teaching focuses on developing specific skills that students can apply in real-world situations. This approach emphasizes practical, hands-on learning experiences rather than theoretical knowledge alone. Here are some key aspects of skill-based teaching:

1. **Practical Application:** Lessons are designed to be directly applicable to real-world tasks. For example, in a science class, students might conduct experiments rather than just reading about them.
2. **Active Learning:** Students engage in activities that require them to use the skills they are learning. This could include group projects, simulations, or problem-solving exercises.
3. **Assessment of Skills**: Evaluation is based on the demonstration of skills rather than just written tests. This might involve practical exams, portfolios, or performance tasks.
4. **Customization and Differentiation**: Teaching is tailored to meet the individual needs of students, recognizing that they may be at different skill levels and learn in different ways.
5. **Integration of Technology**: Utilizing technology to enhance learning, such as using software tools for simulations, providing online resources for practice, or incorporating multimedia presentations.
6. **Collaboration and Communication**: Encouraging teamwork and communication skills, which are essential for most real-world tasks. Students often work in groups and are required to present their work.

7. **Critical Thinking and Problem Solving**: Fostering these skills by presenting students with complex, open-ended problems that require them to apply what they've learned in innovative ways.
8. **Feedback and Reflection:** Providing ongoing feedback and opportunities for students to reflect on their learning process and outcomes, helping them to improve continuously.

Skill-based teaching is particularly effective in vocational and technical education, where the primary goal is to prepare students for specific careers. However, it can be applied in any educational context to enhance learning outcomes and better prepare students for future challenges.

4.4-Skill based Teaching

4.4.1 Cycle of skill practice.

Microteaching: Its Meaning

Micro Teaching is an analytical approach to teaching. It is a significant effort to make teacher education program scientific, effective and meaningful. It is now considered not only a constructive teacher training techniques, but also a versatile research tool. It was developed by Prof. Dwight and Robert Bush in teacher preparation program between 1960 and 1967. It may be considered as a miniaturized classroom teaching. It may be stated as a scaled down teaching encounter in class size and class time. The complexity in teaching is reduced by having a small number of students and a short duration of time. The content is also reduced to a single. That is why, one component skill is naturally practiced at one time.

A student teacher teaches a short lesson of five to eight minutes to a small group of pupils, usually five to eight. A single concept is taken up and at the end of the lesson, the pupil leaves and the teacher trainee discuss his lesson with the supervisor. Thereafter, the teacher trainee is given time to think about the discussion and modify his lesson plan accordingly. The student's teacher then reteaches his micro-lesson with a different group of students under the same condition and with the same opportunities for feedback in an attempt to improve his previous lesson. This process of teach-reteach is repeated until the desirable skill is developed and it usually takes about 30-35 minutes.

Time fraction may be considered as below-

To teach- 6 Min
Feedback- 6 Min
Re-plan- 12 Min
Re-teach- 6 Min
Re-feedback- 6 Min
Total- 36 Minutes.

Definitions of Micro-teaching

D, W. Allen: Microteaching is a scaled down teaching encounter in class size and class time.

R.N. Bush: Microteaching is a teacher education technique which allows teacher to apply clearly defined skills to carefully prepared lessons in planned series of 5-10 minutes encounter with a small group of real students, often, with an opportunity to observe the results and videotape.

David B. Young: Microteaching is a device which provides the novice and experienced teacher alike, new opportunities to improve teaching.

J. C. Clift etal: Microteaching is a teacher training procedure which reduces the teaching situation to a simpler and more controlled encounter achieved by limited the practice teaching to a specific skill and reducing teaching time and class size.

Characteristics of Microteaching

1. Objectives are specified in behavioral terms.
2. Class is divided into small groups of 5-10 pupils.
3. Teaching is relatively simple and non-threatening.
4. Immediate feedback is provided by the supervisor.
5. The role of the supervisor is well defined to improve teaching.

6. Patterns of classroom interaction can be objectively studied.
7. The trainee practices only one skill selected for practice.
8. Time duration is 5-10 minutes.
9. It Is a highly individualized training device.
10. There is a high degree of control in practicing a skill.

Objectives of Microteaching

1. To enable the teacher trainee to learn and assimilate new teaching skills under controlled condition.
2. To enable the teacher trainees to gain confidence in training and mastering a number of teaching skills on a small group of pupils.
4. To utilize the academic potential of teacher trainees for providing much needed feedback.
5. To give the teacher trainees training in the component skills of teaching at the pre-service level.
6. To gain maximum advantage with title time, money and material.

Principles of Microteaching

Micro-teaching resolves around certain principles to improve its reach in al round developments of the teacher-

1. **One skill at one time: -** In skills in micro-teaching are targeted one at a time. Training on particular skills is given until it is mastered. Once mastered another skill is targeted next. Thus, micro-teaching ais for one skill at a time.
2. **Small scale content: -** Limiting the content gives more freedom and ease to the trainees. Thus, micro-teaching is based upon the principle of limited content. Teachers are to prepare their lessons within the given content; therefore, it becomes easier for them to conduct their lessons.

3. **Practice:** – Mastering skills require practice. While focusing on one skill at a time, microteaching program also gives an opportunity to practice those skills. Lots of practice can boast the self-confidence and promote in development of teaching skills.
4. **Experiments:** – Experiments are the key factors in any concept. In micro-teaching, many experiments are conducted in order to test the skills of the teachers.
5. **Immediate feedback**: – Micro-teaching consists of teacher-pupil and supervisor as students. Once a session ends, teacher-pupil and supervisors come up with their feedback. This feedback is given instantly after the lesson-plan ends. Thus, it helps in rectify the drawbacks.
6. **Self-Evaluation Opportunities:** – Evaluation plays an important role in any task. In micro-teaching, supervisors conduct various test and thus there are several chances to analyze mistakes.

   Evaluation gives an opportunity to understand the mistake and overcome it. This program includes a session where drawbacks are pointed out along with their solution. Thus, overall improvement becomes an easier target.
7. **Continuous Efforts**: – Acquiring and mastering skill is a slow and ongoing process. Even after mastering a previous skill, one should continually strive for betterment. Continuous efforts make it easier to attain overall development.

Significance of Microteaching

1. It is an excellent way to build up skills and confidence and to experience a wide variety of teaching styles and also learn and practice ways of giving constructive feedback.
2. It trains teaching behaviors and skills in a protective environment and helps in receiving well-intended feedback.
3. It helps in getting an insight into the needs and expectations of students.

4. It provides individualized training with more realistic evidence to students.
5. It provides a democratic type of behavior among faculty members and student teachers.
6. It helps in getting feedback which is not critical but constructive, suggestive and helpful and this helps them in their transmission to school teaching.

Phases of Microteaching

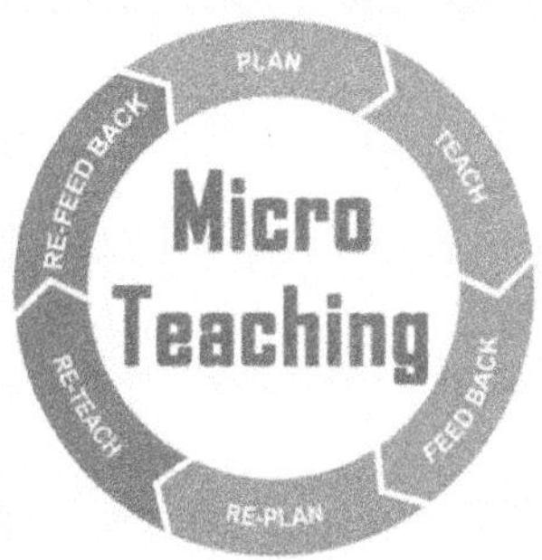

1. **Knowledge Acquisition Phase: -**

   It involves three activities—

   a. To provide knowledge and awareness of a particular teaching skill.

   b. To observe demonstration of the teaching skill.

   c. To analyze and discuss the demonstration of the activities of the skill.

2. **Skill Acquisition Phase: -**

   It also includes three activities—

   a. To prepare a micro lesson for the teaching skill.

   b. To practice a skill in real classroom situation.

   c. To evaluate the preference.

3. **Transfer Phase: -**

   After practicing and acquiring mastery, over a particular skill, the teacher trainees

   are required to transfer the skill in a normal classroom situation.

Components of Microteaching

Microteaching involves four components, which are given below: -

1. Modelling
2. Feedback
3. Microteaching Setting
4. Integration

1. Modelling: Modelling means demonstration of a lesson on the use of a particular skill by the teacher educator or an expert. Modelling includes three types of modelling. These are: –

a. Perceptual Modelling
b. Symbolic Modelling
c. Audio Modelling

- **Perceptual Modelling**: – In perceptual modelling, a film or a videotape or a live model of the derived behaviors of a particular skill is shown. The purpose behind this act is to help acquire the behaviors through imitation.
- **Symbolic Modelling**: – In this format of modelling, written materials in the form of handbooks, guide, materials etc. are presented.
- **Audio Modelling**: – In audio modelling version of the format, the desired behaviors of a skill are presented through audiotape recorder.

2. Feedback: – Feedback is one of the most important components of microteaching. After teaching and re-teaching immediate feedback is provided to the student's trainee in order to modify the behavior in the desired direction. This helps in acquisition of teaching skills. Teaching can also be recorded systematically in an audio or videotape recorder to review the teaching for providing immediate feedback

3. Microteaching Setting: – Microteaching setting refers to a microteaching class which coincide of 5-10 students and the duration of the micro lesson is 5-10 minutes. In the Indian model, duration of micro lesson plan is six minutes. The purpose of microteaching setting is to gain mastery over teaching skill. Microteaching setting facilitates a student trainee to undergo the different steps of a microteaching cycle. The schematic diagrams of microteaching setting and a micro-teaching cycle are given under the heading "Procedure of Implementation" in this unit.

4. Integration of teaching: – Integration of teaching skills mean selection and organization of teaching skills in a real classroom situation through a lesson plan. In analytic approach to teaching, the student's trainee is exposed thoroughly in one teaching skill at a time. After acquisition of that skill, the next skill is taken up for practice. In this way, the student's trainee is trained to integrate the different skills through different strategies.

Steps in Microteaching

1. **Defining the skill (In terms of specific teaching behavior):** – The skills of microteaching are defined regarding the teaching behavior in order to procure knowledge of required skills, which they have to focus on.
2. **Demonstrating the skill by the teacher educator**: – Experts demonstrate the specific skill by themselves or with the help of audio-videotape recordings to the teacher trainee. This gives an idea to the teacher to work accordingly.
3. **Planning the lesson by a teacher trainee**: – The trainee teacher plans a short lesson through which he/she could practice the skill. This microteaching lesson plan is done with the help of his supervisor.
4. **Teaching the Micro lesson**: – Once the lesson planning is done, according to the targeted skill, the pupil teacher teaches the planned lesson to the group of students. These lessons are observed by supervisor and pupil teachers.
5. **Discussion on the lesson delivered**: – Once the teaching session comes to an end, it is followed by a concluding session. Concluding session consists of feedback by the supervisor.

   During this session, the audio or video recording may also be displayed in order to give an opportunity to evaluate oneself. Moreover, it also boosts the confidence level of the trainee.
6. **Re-planning the lesson:** – Mastering a skill is an ongoing process. Thus, once the cycle of micro-teaching revolves, the process is repeated. This repetition involves re-

planning of the lesson-plan. The aim of this re-planning is to master the skill mentioned earlier.

7. **Re-teaching the lesson:** – On completion of the re-planning of the lesson, it is again taught to another group of students from the same class. The time duration is kept as same as the previous class. This method contributes in practicing the skill repeatedly.
8. **Re-discussion or Re-feedback:** – At the end of re-teaching session, the discussion and conclusion step are repeated. These discussion and suggestions encourage the performance of the trainee. Thus, the process of feedback is procured to enhance the performance further more.
9. **Repeating the cycle:** – After the end of every session, this cycle is repeated. The repetition is continued until the required skill is mastered. This process is repeated while attaining all the required skills.

Thus, we can conclude that micro-teaching involves the 4R's viz, Recording, Re-teaching, Re-discussing and Re-doing.

Assumptions of Microteaching

1. It can reduce the complexities of teaching.
2. It develops the teaching skills by integrating theory and practice.
3. It is a successful technique for individualized training.
4. It is useful both at the pre-service as well as in-service education program.
5. Self-evaluation is possible.
6. Provision of immediate and effective feedback.
7. Objectives are specifically and clearly written.
8. Teaching behavior can be objectively studied.
9. The drawbacks in the teaching process can be found out and improved.

Advantages of Microteaching

1. It reduces the complexities of the teaching situations in terms of number of students, time duration and the subject matter.
2. Several reliable and authentic sources are employed for providing necessary feedback.
3. Teaching is performed under simulated conditions with a small group of students and therefore trainee is on a safe practice ground.
4. Since it is an Individualized training technique, each trainee can make progress at his own rate.
5. It focuses attention on teaching behavior with a view to improve and modify.
6. It helps in building confidence and provides continuous reinforcements.
7. The trainee gets many opportunities to study the desire pattern of behavior through demonstration given by the experts and thus he develops his own style of teaching.

Disadvantages of Microteaching

1. It is skill oriented rather than content oriented.
2. It is time consuming.
3. It presents a fragmented view of teaching.
4. It is not possible for a trainee to receive training in evaluation, diagnostic and remedial skill.
5. It does not allow for the creativity of the teacher.
6. It can be carried on successfully only in a controlled environment, whereas classroom situations are flexible.
7. It may not fit in Indian conditions, and may create administrative and academic problems.
8. It cannot work in isolation and should be used along with other techniques.

Comparison Between Microteaching and Traditional Teaching

1. **Simple vs Complex Teaching: -** Microteaching has been more or less simple and non-threatening. traditional teaching has been relatively complex and threatening.
2. **Duration:** – In micro-teaching, the duration is usually 5-10 minutes. In traditional teaching, the duration is 40-6-minutes.
3. **Pattern of Class-room interaction:** – In micro-teaching, it is possible to study patterns of classroom interaction objectively. In traditional teaching, patterns of classroom interaction cannot be objectively studied.
4. **Specification of Objective:** – in microteaching, objectives can be specified in terms of behavioral pattern. In traditional teaching, the objectives cannot be specified in behavioral terms.
5. **Providing Feedback:** – In microteaching, immediate feedback could be provided. But in traditional teaching, feedback could not be provided.
6. **Size of the class:** – In microteaching, class has been divided into small groups of 5-10 pupil-teachers. in traditional teaching, the class is having 50-100 pupil-teachers.
7. **Awareness**: – Microteaching is able to build more awareness among student teachers with regard to professional training. In traditional teaching, it is not so.
8. **Score:** – Microteaching results yield better score in university examination than their counterpart in conventional teaching.
9. **Practicing Skills:** – In micro-teaching, pupil teacher is able to practice only one selected skill for practice. In traditional teaching, pupil teacher is able to practice whole complex teaching behavior.
10. **Role of Supervisor:** – In micro-teaching, the role of supervisor is highly specific and well defined or improving lesson teaching. In conventional teaching, the

role of supervisor has been more or less vague and not useful to improve teaching.

4.4.2 Skill of writing instructional objectives.

If we think instruction is a simple task, it may be possible to list all the types of behavior directly and to include them all in evaluation of student performance. At the end of instruction, this is characteristic of the teaching-learning process at the training level. For higher levels of instruction, however, it-is possible to list only sample of the specific types of behavior which representative of instructional objectives and these guide teaching learning process and testing. But instruction is not only depending on small sample of behavior it includes larger domain of behavior. So, learning outcomes in higher level should have two step-process.

1. To state the instructional objectives as general learning out comes.
2. To list under each object specific sample of behavior which is an indicator of the attainment of objective.

Meaning of Instructional Objectives

Instructional objectives are statements of specific outcomes of instruction that intends to bring out desired behaviour or performance among the students. They are related to goals but their specificity is needed to plan and evaluate instruction.

General Instructional Objectives

The first step in defining instructional objectives is to state the general learning outcomes we expect from our teaching. While writing general objectives the following points are to be kept in mind.

a. Begin each general instructional objective with a verb. (knows, understands, appreciates, etc.,) (For example, students apply the knowledge of motion to day-to-day life situation)
b. State each objective in terms of student performance.
c. State each objective as learning product
d. State the objective so that it includes only one general learning outcome.

e. State each objective so that it indicates terminal behaviour

f. State each objective at the proper level of generality. It should indicate the expected learning outcome and is readily definable by specific types of student behaviour experiences. They give directions to evaluation the learning experience provided to students. Psychology is the basis of instructional objectives. Instructional objectives are very specific which bring desirable change among the students.

They are beginning steps for educational objectives.

The teacher's work becomes more systematic in teaching and evaluation of students. So instructional objectives are inevitable for the teachers as educationists without these they will be blind planners in education ventures.

1. Objectives worth pursuing can be more distinguished from those not worth pursuing when specific outcomes are indicated.
2. Teachable and learning elements related to goals can be identified and arranged in instructional sequences.
3. Individual needs of students and special needs of groups of students can be identified, planned for and evaluated more effectively.
4. Learning activities and instructional materials can be selected and used to attain clearly defined out comes.
5. Evaluation of outcomes of instruction can be improved because observable behavior or a product of behavior is specified.
6. Desired outcomes of instruction can be communicated more effectively to students and to parents.
7. The operation of accountability programs can be improved because clearly defined objectives are specified, and
8. Policy making can be facilitated because more adequate data on educational needs and the strengths and weaknesses of instruction are provided. Instructional objectives should be viewed as tools that are useful in improving teaching and learning process.

Taxonomy of Instructional Objectives by Bloom-A Bird's Eye view

The word "Taxonomy of Instructional Objectives" is closely related with the name B.S. Bloom. He has explained them extraordinarily in 1956. It is accepted by teachers, educationists and test developers. It also offers systematic evaluation of the whole range of cognitive processes and its impact on curriculum development and teaching methods. It further lays emphasis on processes rather than contents.

It has maintained the proper balance between lower and higher cognitive process. Bloom's **Taxonomy has inspired the majority of other taxonomies uses four basic principles.**

a. The major distinction should reflect the ways teachers state educational objectives (methodological principle).

b. The taxonomy should be consistent with our present understanding of psychological phenomena (Psychological principle).

c. The taxonomy should be logically developed and internally consistent (logical principles).

d. The hierarchy of objectives does not correspond to hierarchy of values (objective principle). The taxonomy itself comprises six cognitive levels.

Hierarchy

Knowledge ⟶ Comprehension ⟶ Application ⟶

Analysis ⟶ Synthesis ⟶ Evaluation ⟶

1.Knowledge is defined as recall of specifics and universal which is lowest level in cognitive development.

2.Comprehension involves understanding or previewing which means processing of information.

3.Application involves using something in a specific manner.

4.Analysis - involved breaching down or the separation of a whole into its component parts.

5.Synthesis - it is apposite to analysis. It involves combining together a number of demerits in order to form a coherent whole.

6.Evaluation - It is highest level in the taxonomy which is combination of all the 5 categories which is concerned with making judgement about value.

NCERT Classification System

National Council for Educational Research and Training established was in New Delhi in 1961. It classified educational objectives into three main categories which are condensed form of Bloom's "Taxonomy".

1.Knowledge2.Understanding/Comprehension,

3. Applications

The specifications of these objectives are

1. Knowledge: The pupil
   - i. Recalls
   - ii. Recognizes
2. Understanding / Comprehension: The pupil
   - a) Translates
   - b) Identifies
   - c) relationship
   - d) Compares
   - e) Interprets
   - f) Cites examples
   - g) Detects error
   - h) Classifies
   - i) Explains
3. Application: The pupil
   - a) Analyses
   - b) Suggests methods and materials
   - c) Hypothesizes
   - d) Establishes relationships
   - e) Reasons out
   - f) Generalizes or draws conclusions.
   - g) Predicts
   - h) Judges' adequacy,
   - i) consistency and relevance etc.

Criteria for a well stated instructional objectives

As you know, the objectives should be stated properly in well-defined terms and clear language. The criteria for a well-stated instructional objective.

Aspects

a. Object: Specification of the content, concepts skills attitude or other instructional objectives which is the focus of the objective and instruction what is being studied? What is the focus of instructional objective?

b. Specification of Leaner: the objective must specifically indicate the learner to whom, the objectives were written for i.e. who is going to demonstrate change in behaviour on end product of the instruction.

c. Specification of learner performances in observable behavioral terms (using verbs in writing objectives that indicate behaviour that are observed directly).

d. Specification of the conditions in which the learner performance occurs (learning experiences, provided for the-students rural tools/materials are needed to demonstrate understanding.

e. Specification of minimum expected level of performance of the learner: Specification of how well students must perform the behaviour with a set of conditions. What is the criterion of acceptable performance (i.e. 85%, 90%, 100%). What level of accuracy, proficiency, or speed must the student attain to meet the objective?

f. Time: Designation of time by which students will be expected to meet the objectives when should the objective be attained? By the end of unit? By end of term? By the end of Lesson? By end of week?

g. Covering objectives of all the three domains cognitive, affective and psychomotor.

h. Covering objectives of different levels of learning out-come

i. Formulating objectives of instruction in direct relation with the particular content of the lesson.

j. Correlating objectives with evaluation procedure

Example-1: At the end of the unit, the students will be able to write in tabulated form a essay on the role of different enzymes in the digestion of food giving the source, food rested upon, organs associated and resulting end products.

a. Object: Role of different enzymes in digestion and
b. Learner: All students
c. Observable behaviour term: will be able to write
d. Conditions: In a tabulated form
e. Minimum expected level of performance: In the digestion of food giving the source, food reacted upon, organs associated and resulting end products.
f. Time: By the end of the unit

Example 2: By the end of period given out line map of India, with points representing major cities marked and list of ten major cities the IX Standard students will be able to Label nine out of ten cities correctly.

a. Object: Major cities in India
b. Learner: IX Standard students
c. Behavioral term: will be able to label
d. Conditions: Give an outline map with points of major cities
e. Minimum expected level of performance: 9 out 10 major cities correctly
f. Time: by the end of a period

Guidelines for Writing Instructional Objectives (Knowledge, Understanding, Application, Skills etc.

1. Keep in mind the entry behaviour of learner.
2. Give thought to the element of content, topic or the learning experience to be provided to the learner.
3. Keep in mind the teaching-learning objective.
4. Select appropriate mental processor abilities for writing objectives. For writing objectives as knowledge, understanding, application, skill mental process and abilities involved should be used.

   For example.:

1. Knowledge

a. The students will be able to recognize

b. The students will be able to recall

2. Understanding

The student will be able to-

(a) to see relationship, between and,

(b) to discriminate between and

(c) to classify,

(d) to interpret,

(f) to generalize,

(g) to cite example.

3. Application The student will be able to –

(a) reason,

(b) formulate,

(c) establish,

(d) infer,

(e) predict.

4. Skills The student will be able to –

(a) drawing skill,

(b) manipulative skills

4.4.3 Skill of Introducing a Lesson

When we meet a person, group we usually start a conversation with a primary talk. The nature of the induction determines the effectiveness of the conversation and relationship bond between the two. In the classroom also, at the very beginning a teacher has to refine the mood of students and make them relax and ready to learn. It can be possible only a nice introduction of the lesson. The skill of a teacher to introduce a lesson is called Skill of introducing a lesson. This skill is also called the skill of set induction. The skill helps the teacher to attract the students' attention towards class lessons. It motivates students to learn, a good introduction assists the teacher to create a disequilibrium in the brain of the student and thereby arouses a curiosity to learn. Moreover, it helps to link the student's previous knowledge with new knowledge to be presented before them. Let us discuss the component behaviour of the skill of introducing a lesson

Component Behaviour

Component behavior are the essential constituting elements of a skill which make a skill perfect. These are the essential criteria or index points where a teacher should necessarily follow while practicing a particular skill. The component behaviors of the skill of introducing a lesson are given below.

- **Use of previous knowledge of the students**
  The knowledge that the students already have related to the lesson should be checked or used while introducing the lesson. It will help the learner to easily hook the new learning material to the previous one, where the learning process becomes very easy, effective as well as retentive.
- **Use of appropriate supporting aids, devices or techniques**
  To make introductions interesting and effective, teachers should use appropriate devices like bulletin boards, video clips, newspaper, Pictures, TV news, Questioning, Narration, Storytelling, Demonstration, Dramatization, role playing, imaginary conversation, travelogue and so on.
- **Arousing Motivation and create interest**
  Teacher conversation and Presentation of learning material and supporting aids should be in motivating nature and thereby create interest among the students to go forward for further classroom transaction.
- **Ensure the relevancy**
  Introduction should be relevant to the content of the lesson, situation, time and mental age of the students. So, selection of the introducing material, technique is crucial one.
- **Link with previous knowledge and content part**
  Teachers should connect the previous knowledge of the student with the learning content to be taught effectively.

Teachers should plan the introduction part in a manner that helps the students to make connections with previous knowledge and content parts. So present the introduction in sequential and logical order

- **Continuity and smooth transition**

  Maintaining continuity of the presentation is vital to retain the concentration and attention of the student in the class. By keeping the flow of the presentation, the teacher should smoothly cross the introduction and start the lesson. Students should not feel the difference between introduction and the lesson presentation.

4.4.4 - Skill of explaining (Narration)

This is an important skill that teachers should possess. Explanation is the core activity of every classroom interaction irrespective of the teaching strategy a teacher follows. A teacher with good explaining ability can make wonders in the classroom. Explanation skill helps the teacher to understand their learners about the concept, idea, facts, principle etc., clearly and meaningfully. Generally, a teacher explains when he describes 'how' 'why' and 'what' of a concept, phenomenon or event.

Component Behavior

The detailed description of the component behaviour of skill of explaining is presented below

1. **Use of appropriate beginning statements**

   First component behaviour is to start the explanation with a beginning statement. Before starting the explanation, teacher should make an appropriate beginning statement to attract the attention of the learners to the topic. Beginning statement is an opening statement announcing what is going to be explained by the teacher. Such as saying that now we will discuss the causes of the first war of Indian independence, let us explain the causes of the First World War, etc.

2. **Use of Explaining Links**

   To make explanations more meaningful the teacher has to use the words or phrases which may Link/continuity between the sentences and thereby increase the effectiveness of explanation. Teachers can use explaining links such as, hence, as a result of, therefore, in order, because, as soon as, due to, that is why etc. while explaining any events of phenomenon.

3. **Use of Mediator**

   Sometimes teachers need supporting aids to make explanations simpler and more effective. For this very purpose teachers can use the teaching aids like pictures, graphs, charts, video clips etc. these are called mediators in classroom teaching.

4. **Covering essential points**

   Explanation is meant for bringing more clarity regarding the topic discussed. Hence Teacher should ensure that all the essential points in the topic have been included in the classroom discussion. Pedagogic analysis helps the teacher to identify the all-essential points in a lesson.

5. **Fluency and clarity**

   Explanation should be very clear, avoid unnecessary things which may bring misconception among the learners. Ensure the flow of the points and sentences without any extended delay throughout the lesson.

6. **Use simple language**

   The ultimate purpose of the explanation is to make the concept or phenomena clear to learners. It has been observed that some teachers are using literary languages which may not be digestive to the brain of the students. It should be noted that a teacher should not use indigestive literary words to exhibit his/her language proficiency. Teachers should explain the content using very simple and easy language that can be understood by the learner.

7. **Testing Pupils' Understanding**

   While explaining the topic the teacher has to take feedback through possible tests. Teachers can ask questions or use any other evaluation technique to understand whether the students have understood the concept or principle and thereby retain or change their explanation style further.

8. **Use of Concluding Statements**

   At the end of the explanation Teacher has to put a concluding remark about the topic and explanation. It will help the learner to hook the learned content in a particular schema in an integrated manner. So, the teacher has to conclude the explanation with appropriate concluding statements soon after s/he completes the explanation. For example, these are the reasons for the first world war. We have completed the discussion of reasons for the first world war. Let us recall once again what we have discussed now etc. It will help the learner to concrete their learning in the cognitive domain.

4.4.5 -Skill of Stimulus Variation.

Children perceive the objects in their environment or in a situation (known as stimulus) and select the relevant information depending on the intensity, contrast and the movement of the objects. The children's attention is drawn through attractive objects, the contrast between the two objects tends to attract their attention. Continuous use of the same stimulus for a long period reduces the attention in that activity. The teacher's behaviour influences pupil's attention. Variation in stimulus secures more attention among the students. He/she should present multiple stimuli just to gain the attention of students for the purpose of facilitating learning. In other words, for optimum learning the teacher uses a variety of stimuli in the chosen instructional tasks. In these stimuli, the teacher should himself function as a stimulus, in the form of gestures, movements of the body, change in voice, change in interaction styles, pausing and sequencing of different aids of teaching etc. All these aspects act as stimuli in the class.

The effective use of these stimuli during teaching is known as skill of stimulus variation.

Following are the main components of the skill of stimulus variation.

1. Teacher's Physical Movements
2. Pupils' Physical Participation
3. Teacher's Gestures
4. Change in Voice
5. Focusing
6. Change in the Interaction Styles
7. Pausing and

Oral -Visual Switching Component-wise description of skill of stimulus variation is given below.

1. **Teacher's Physical Movements**: Teacher's physical movement during teaching in the classroom serves a pedagogic purpose. Purposeful movements of the teacher keep the students attentive to what is being discussed. Purposeful or relevant movements include: moving towards blackboard to discuss the diagram or to write important points, moving to display and explain teaching aids, movement to check student's activities or help them in solving certain problems etc. The movements of the teacher secure and maintain attention of the students.
2. **Pupils' Physical Participation**: The teacher should encourage and ensure active participation of the students. The physical participation holds pupil's interest and attention in the task in which they are engaged. They should be given the opportunity to actually handle the apparatus, set-up and conduct experiments with all possible precautions, allowing to write their correct answer on the blackboard, dramatization etc. By doing so, we can sustain their interest even for higher level learning.
3. **Teacher's Gestures**: Expression of feelings and emotions involving non-verbal behaviours are called gestures. The teacher's gestures in the class can motivate or demotivate the students in their learning. The teacher's actions and expression can have a direct bearing on his students' learning. Use of gestures increases the effectiveness of verbal communication. Gestures consist of head and hand movements, movement of eyes, body movements and facial

expressions, etc. Gestures are used to emphasize ideas, indicate shape/ size (like big, small, straight, circular etc), pointing from student to student, nodding, smiling, looking thoughtfully at the students, thoughtful mood, acceptance or rejection etc. There should always be a perfect coordination between the verbal communication and the appropriate/relevant corresponding gestures.

4. **Change in Voice:** The teacher's voice dominates the entire class. Voice of the teacher has several dimensions namely pitch, tone and speed. Communication with constant use of the same level of pitch, tone and speed by the teacher makes his communication dull, inactive and students feel boredom. So, the teachers should modulate their voice. Teacher should bring about a change in his voice. Too high or too low pitch should be avoided. Important points should be stressed by changing the pitch of the voice.
5. **Focusing:** It is very important to lay stress on some specific points or events. This process of focusing includes:
   - Verbal Focusing: Verbal focusing draws the attention of the students by using certain verbal statements/words like listen it is an important aspect; all students will now look at the chart etc.
   - Gesture Focusing: Gesture focusing draws their attention by pointing finger/pointer at teaching aid, written words or pictures etc. It includes indicating an important part in working model through pointe etc.
   - Verbal-cum-Gesture Focusing: The use of verbal statements and gestures simultaneously to stress on some specific aspects are known as verbal-cum-gesture focusing. Verbal-cum-gesture focusing is termed as sensory focus. Like showing some concrete object along with stressing on it's functioning.
6. **Change in the Interaction Styles:** In a classroom, interaction between students and teacher is must otherwise the classroom environment will become monotonous. This interaction is nothing but communication. But this

interaction should be different. The main patterns of interaction between teacher and pupils are teacher-pupil interaction, teacher- group interaction, pupil-pupil interaction, and teacher-whole class interaction. All these types of interactions can be arranged by teachers. A teacher should ask questions in an interactive manner so that his class becomes more interesting and effective. The teacher should introduce variation in the interaction patterns to secure and maintain pupils' attention.

7. **Pausing**: Pausing is silence for few seconds. The silence indicates pause during talk. Silence has a meaning of its own and if it is used effectively, it helps in securing and sustaining pupils' attention. There should be regular pauses during the process of explanation in the class. A short pause before saying something important is an effective way of attracting pupils' attention. A pause of 3 seconds duration is considered appropriate for this purpose. If the pause is unduly long, it loses its effectiveness in serving pupils' attention. Appropriate pausing time, response time of the student to the teacher's question as well as change from one concept to another is 3 seconds.
8. **Oral -Visual Switching**: Visual medium can be in the form of showing a chart, pictures, graph, map, and model or in the form of drawing pictures, figures and graphs on the black board. But the oral medium can be in the form of speech only. Only oral medium or only visual medium creates boredom in the class. A teacher should vary his medium in order to secure and sustain attention i.e. from audio to visual, visual to audio, audio or visual to audio visual. Various means of communication can be combined according to the chosen objectives of the lesson. The use of oral visual media will provide multi-sensory stimuli to the students.

Precautions while practicing skill of stimulus variation.

- Body movements should be in balance because their excessive use may distract students and similarly less body movements will make the teacher look like a dull statue.

- Avoid aimless and habitual wandering and pacing up and down the class.
- Avoid continue talking in class endlessly. If the teacher speaks continuously, students would get bored.
- Teaching aids will serve their purpose only when it is prepared properly, displayed at appropriate time and explained effectively.

4.4.6- Skill of illustrating with examples

Explain the concepts with examples and accelerate the understanding of learners. We have seen such teachers giving life-oriented examples while taking the classes. This skill should be developed among all teachers to produce effective teaching. Students Understanding will be more effective when the teacher uses examples to explain facts, principles, generalization, concepts etc in the lesson. Selection of relevant examples and its proper illustration at proper time is an art from the part of teachers. Students are more interestingly attending the class of teachers who teach with life-oriented examples.

Component Behaviour

The following are the component behaviour of the skill of illustrating with examples

1. **Use Relevant Examples**

   Select relevant examples related to concepts being explained. Examples should be exactly matching with the content, context. Teacher should not use the example which create confusion among the students

2. **Use Simple Examples**

   Use simple and digestive examples in the classroom. Simple examples are those examples which are based on the pupils' life surroundings and their past experiences. Extreme care should be taken while selecting the example to be suit with their level of maturity.

3. **Use Interesting Examples**
   Examples should not be merely for the sake of example. It should create interest among the students. If a teacher succeeds in attracting the attention of the students towards his example illustration and thereby students are able to comprehend the concept, idea and principle clearly; the example is said to be interesting.
4. **Use appropriate Media**
   Exemplifying can be done through verbal or non-verbal media like storytelling, analogy, concrete objects, maps, pictures, models and experimental demonstration. Teachers can select the most appropriate media for Exemplifying as per the situation and content.
5. **Use genuine example**
   Examples should be genuine so that it enhances the retention power of the learner. Students should not feel that teachers are manipulating something for teaching the content. That may divert the attention of the students towards genuineness of the example and the content of example rather than the base content.
6. **Use of Inductive-Deductive Approach**
   This deals with how a teacher can illustrate an example related to content. Teachers can either use an inductive approach for illustrating with examples that means starting from particular examples to generalization or deductive approach in which the teacher first explains the generalized concept and the site the particular examples of the concept.

4.4.7- Skill of probing questions

We have discussed the skill of fluency in asking questions. When the students are asked questions in the classroom, they give various types of responses as per their knowledge and situation. It may be incorrect, partially correct or completely correct. In the case of incorrect or partially correct responses teachers have to lead students to the correct responses or right answers. For this very purpose teachers have to go further and probe into their responses by asking a number of supplementary questions on what they already know. This process may lead them to the correct responses. On the other hand, even if the response is correct, the teacher has to motivate them to further query for depth knowledge in the area of discussion. An action of probing students towards a better and broader perspective of the response by asking further depth questions. The technique that deals with student response, going deep into students' knowledge by asking a series of questions is called probing question. Skill of probing questions is a specialized skill that should be acquired by all teachers who are keen to become an effective teacher.

Component Behaviour

The components behaviour of the skill of probing questions are given below.

1. **Prompting:** It is the act of giving clues or hints to the students for leading the pupil to the desired responses when they give incorrect or partially correct answers to the question. For example, when the students responded as subhash Chandra Bose to a question, who led the Non-Cooperation movement in India. Teachers can give clues like, see he is our father of the nation, He was born in Gularath , Porbanther etc.
2. **Seeking Further Information**

   When the students give partial or incomplete responses to the questions the teacher has to seek further information regarding answers given by students. It will lead the students to arrive at correct desired responses. Suppose the teacher asked the students what the different types of pollution are. Students give a partially correct answer like, water pollution, air pollution. Then the teacher seeks further information like, 1) Do you like to go for a tour into a natural park? 2) why? 3)How do you feel when you hear the sound or severe horn sound of vehicles? 4) Why? 5) Is there any problem related to noise? 6) Can we call it pollution? 7) what type of pollution?

3. **Refocusing**

   It is the technique of a teacher to strengthen the correct responses given by the students to a question. When the pupils give the correct responses the teacher once again briefly explains the same by relating their responses with something already taught or known to the learners.

4. **Redirection**

   It is an act of sustaining all students to be vigilant in the classroom. Teachers should ask the same question to the several students sitting at different corners of the classroom. It will help the learners to be vigilant and attentive in the classroom. In the process the teacher can get feedback as well as select an accurate response among the various responses to the question.

5. **Increasing critical awareness**

   One of the purposes of questioning is to create critical awareness among the students. To increase the critical awareness ability among the students, teachers should ask supplementary questions framed by 'why' and 'how' for correct responses given by the students. For example, Teacher asked a question to the students about what are the Gandian principles. Students responded that Ahimsa, Noncooperation, Truth etc. teacher again asked Do you think that the Principle Ahimsa was a correct step taken by Gandhi, why?

4.4.8 - Skill of fluency of questioning

Fluency and good delivery of questions in classroom is an integral part of the skill of questioning. The rate of meaningful questions put per unit time by the teacher is called fluency of questioning. Meaningful questions are those which are relevant to the concept being taught, are well structured and delivered effectively (from communication point of view). There are three components of the skill related to fluency and delivery of questions:

I)Structure. II)Process & III) Product

I) Structure: You should how the technique of structuring the question to suit the requirement of the students and the concepts being taught. Structuring of the question is in fad a technique of formulation of questions. The content and language used play an important role in framing and delivering the questions. The content part of a question refers to the subject matter and its language part refers to the following five aspects.

a) Grammatical correctness

b) Conciseness

c) Relevancy

d) Specificity, and

e) Clarity

Let us elaborate each of these five aspects with the help of suitable examples.

a) Grammatical correctness: You as a teacher, are expected to use grammatically correct, unambiguous and simple language. Carelessly used language creates confusion. Students will take more time to understand md respond to a question if it is improperly worded. Such a practice will create hindrance in fluency and good delivery of your questions, and this will reduce your effectiveness and hold up the progress of your students.

Here are two simple examples of wrongly worded questions and their correct versions:

- Where is Rani Durgawati born ? (Wrong)
- Where was Rani Durgawati born? (Correct)
- Where did Olympic games started? (Wrong)
- Where did the Olympic games originate? (Correct)

b) Conciseness: Conciseness refers to the minimal but essential length of a question. A question should be direct and straight forward about the content; it should be concise and free from redundancy. Teachers often use more words than are necessary in their questions. Extra words should, be always avoided because very long questions or questions that have more words than are necessary make communication less effective; they confuse and bore students.

The following examples will help you understand the importance of proper use of words while framing a question.

- Incorrect: Does anybody in the class how, when India became a Republic?
- Correct: When did India become a Republic?

You have seen that the first question contains extra words which should have been avoided. At the same time, we should not be miserly in the use of necessary words. A question cannot be treated as a telegram with minimum words. A good question should always contain the appropriate number of words. It should convey whatever is intended to be conveyed: it should convey neither more or less.

c) Relevance: As has already been mentioned, your question should be relevant to the content and the context. Besides, the questions should suit the mental level of your students. The ultimate objective is to use questions as a tool for effective teaching and learning. The teacher should be able to teach better and the learners learn better. Questions which are not related to the topic being taught are irrelevant and they confuse students. Use of terms which are beyond the knowledge of students is also irrelevant. A good question should use only such terms which are understood by the students.

d) Specificity: The question should be specific to the content and should call for a single answer. Example - Which is the adjective in this sentence? Which is the longest river of the world?

e) Clarity: As the term indicates, clarity in terms of content and language is an essential component of questioning skill. Clarity increases the fluency and delivery of questions. If a question is not clear enough, it will lead to misinterpretation and as a result a teacher will have to provide necessary explanation or clarification.

II) Process: The process of formulating and asking question has more than one aspect/component. There are four major components of skills related to the process of questioning. These are: speed, voice, pause and style.

We shall elaborate each of these components with the help of suitable illustrations.

1) Speed of asking questions: You should not ask question at a slow speed, in pieces or hurriedly. Very slow speed of questioning decreases the fluency of questioning and is a time-consuming activity. Very hurriedly asked questions do not provide any clear idea about the intention of the teacher and may become difficult for students to understand the question and to respond to it. Question asked with unnecessary pauses also create hindrance in the way of its proper understanding. See the following examples:

- How many months are there in a year ? (asked very rapidly)
- How .... many .... months .... a .... a year? (too slow)
- How .... many months ...... tell me Kamala are there .... in a year ? (in pieces1i.e. fragments)

2) Voice: While asking questions your voice should be audible and clear enough so that every student understands the question properly. You should ask questions in a slightly raised voice to enable the students sitting at the back to hear you. By doing so, you can also detect those students who are hard of hearing or have some hearing problems.

3) Pause: Pause is defined as the time or the period of silence given by teacher just after the delivery of the question to the class. Pause helps the students understand and think about the question and formulate its answer. Pause enable students 'to understand the intention of the teacher about the level of the answer he expects of the students. The length of the pause depends on the type of the question asked. However, the guidelines for pauses are as follows:

- Short pause for memory level answers.
- Relatively longer pause for answers to higher order questions.

A pause after the interrogative words such as 'who', 'which', 'where', gives stress on the expected correct response.

4) Style: You should take care that the question should be put using a style suitable for questioning and in a declaration style which is used for statements. The question should be asked in a properly modulated and pleasant tone and friendly manner.

Besides observing the above-mentioned components of the skill of fluency and delivery of questions, you should take precaution to avoid unnecessary repetition of a question. The repetition of a question leads to wastage of rime and this practice encourages students to be inattentive. Therefore, you should not repeat a question unless it is necessary to do so. This is important in order to maintain fluency of questioning.

III) Product

The product means the student's answer to the question asked by the teacher question followed by answer; is an effective strategy for sustaining the teaching learning process. The product of questioning depends on various factors. Chief among these are following:

- The students may not be intelligent enough to understand the question you have asked.
- The language of the question may be of a higher difficulty level for students.
- The students may not be taking interest in your class.
- The students may be inattentive in your class or may be disturbed by the noise in the environinent, or there may be lack of rapport between the teacher (you) and the students.

In all these situations you should re-examine your teaching strategies and find out the cause of students' non-response. Once you are sure about the cause (s), you can decide upon the remedial mechanism to be used. You can explore the reasons as to why they are non-responsive to the questions asked. You can also observe the students' behaviour and find out the factors (such as fatigue, disturbing physical environment, etc) responsible for their passive behaviour and non-response. You can even undertake action research in order to make your teaching more effective and result-oriented.

4.4.9 - Skill of reinforcement

Reinforcement denotes an event that influences the probability of a response to a stimulus being produced under similar conditions. It belongs to the psychology of learning. It is of two types: positive and negative. Use of positive reinforcement contributes towards strengthening the desirable responses or behaviour and use of negative reinforcement contributes towards eliminating undesirable responses. Reinforcement is not only used to promote learning, but also to secure attention and provide greater motivation to the students. For this, the academic activities should be meaningful and worthwhile so that the students can get the intended benefits from them. If the students' behaviour is approved by the class teacher, they feel motivated to participate with enthusiasm and take initiative in instructional activities.

The skill of reinforcement can be developed by using the following components.

1. Positive Verbal Reinforcement
2. Positive Non-Verbal Reinforcement
3. Extra Verbal Cues
4. Repeating and Rephrasing Student's Responses and
5. Writing Student's Answers on Blackboard

Component-wise description of skill of reinforcement is given below.

1. **Positive Verbal Reinforcement:** This type of reinforcement strengthens the probability of occurrence of correct responses by the students. It involves the use of verbal or linguistic expressions (praise words) after the correct response of the students like yes, right, good, very good, excellent, splendid, correct, well done, fantastic, go on, go ahead, carry on, continue etc. The use of type of reinforcers depends on the maturity of the learner and quality of response.

2. **Positive Non-Verbal Reinforcement**: It includes teacher's gestures conveying pleasant feelings or approval of student's responses like smiling, nodding of head for acceptance, a delightful laugh, clapping, keeping eyes on the responding student, giving ear to the student's response, contact with the student by way of patting, giving him an encouraging look etc. It involves the use of teacher's gestures in order to reinforce the student's behaviour.
3. **Extra Verbal Cues**: Teacher's utterances like 'aha', 'humm-humm' etc., can encourage the **students to continue with his answer and to arrive at the correct response.**
4. **Repeating and Rephrasing Student's Responses:** The important point(s)/correct responses made by the student can be re-emphasized or highlighted by the teacher. 5. Writing Student's Answers on Blackboard: Writing student's original and correct responses on the blackboard encourages him/her to participate in classroom activities and act as a positive reinforcement.

Precautions while practicing the skill of reinforcement

Precautions while practicing the skill of reinforcement are as follows.

1. **Negative Verbal Reinforcement**: This type of reinforcement decreases the probability of occurrence of correct responses by the pupils and also reduces their participation in classroom activities. Teacher's statements and the use of discouraging words like no, wrong, incorrect, foolish, shut up, stop it, nonsense, try something else, I don't like what you are doing, do not do like this, that is not good, you don't know even this, etc. correspond to negative verbal reinforcements. Avoid making use of negative verbal reinforcement while teaching.
2. **Negative Non-Verbal Reinforcement**: On some occasions, a teacher uses negative non-verbal reinforcements like angry glares, threat of a slap, frowning, raising the eye brows, staring, disapproval by hands, nodding the head sideway, not looking at the responding pupil, moving away

from the responding pupil, tapping foot impatiently etc. Such negative non-verbal reinforcements affect students learning adversely and should be avoided.

3. **Wrong Use of Reinforcement**: It includes instances where reinforcement was given, but it was not required at that moment.
4. **Inappropriate Use of Reinforcement:** It includes such encouraging remarks, which are not made according to the quality of the response of the pupil. A teacher will provide reinforcement after analyzing the quality and level of the correct response made by the students. Try to avoid making use of same type of reinforcer for every response.
5. **Excessive use of reinforcement:** Excessive use of reinforcement should be avoided. It may remove its effectiveness. Positive reinforcement should be used for all the students and not only for the intelligent ones.

4.4.10 - Skill of using black board

Blackboard is the powerful teaching aid to teach from pre-primary to higher levels of education. Blackboard is a basic visual teaching aid. The development of information and communication technology is reducing the blackboard work by replacing with smart board, interactive boards and other multi-media internet connected boards. Still, it is the most suitable for giving a holistic picture of the lesson. A good blackboard work brings clarity in perception and it can be suitably used for displaying key teaching elements and diagrams during a lesson. The scientific way of using blackboard in teaching-learning process to facilitate learning is termed as the skill of using blackboard.

The components of the skill of blackboard writing are given below.

1. Legibility
2. Size and Alignment
3. Continuity and Highlighting Main Points
4. Utilization of the Space

5. Correctness
6. Position of the Teacher
7. Eye Contact with Pupils
8. Appropriateness of the Figures/ Diagrams and
9. Cleaning of Blackboard

Component-wise description of skill of using Backboard is given below.

1. **Legibility**: The writing is said to be legible if there is maximum ease in reading it. Legible handwriting of the teacher on the blackboard draws the attention of the learners and encourages them to improve their handwriting. Illegible handwriting irritates the learners and results in maximum mistakes, creating misconceptions and improper understanding of the concepts. The teacher should ensure that a clear distinction between every letter. Adequate space should be maintained between individual letters and words etc., to make handwriting more legible.
2. **Size and Alignment**: In blackboard writhing the size and alignment of the letters is very important. The size of the letters on the blackboard should not only be uniform but also the size of the letters should be adequate and large enough to be read by the students sitting in the last row. The size of the capital letters should be as nearly vertical as possible without being diverged from a line. Size of the capital letters should be just bigger than that of the small letters. The sentences should be straight and not going up or down across the blackboard.
3. **Continuity and Highlighting Main Points:** The blackboard work should have continuity which means that a point should be logically related to the previous point. The salient points of the lesson, one after the other as and when they are introduced are to be written on the blackboard in order to facilitate learning. The teacher should underline or highlight the main points or important words on the blackboard. Coloured chalks should be used suitably to draw the learner's attention on the main points.

4. **Utilization of the Space**: For the proper utilization of the space important words or statements should be written on the blackboard. Overwriting on the letters should be avoided as it makes the blackboard work untidy. Only essential material should be retained on the blackboard and unnecessary words should be rubbed off. In Mathematics and Science, try to divide the blackboard in two parts for different purposes like space for rough work/ diagrams etc.
5. **Correctness:** The teacher should be careful about correct spelling, punctuation, grammar etc. in constructing sentences on the blackboard. While writing on the blackboard, inadequate knowledge of grammar or mistakes done by the teacher reduces the attentiveness of the learners in the classroom.
6. **Position of the Teacher:** At the time of writing, the teacher should stand on one side of the blackboard with an angle of 45 degrees, so that the written work on the blackboard is visible to the learners. This means the teacher's position should not be in between the learners and the blackboard. The position should be such that a minimum cross-section of teacher's body is in the students' line of sight.
7. **Eye Contact with Pupils**: The teacher should maintain frequent eye contact with his learners at the time of writing on the blackboard. This controlling interaction maintains discipline and sustains the attention of the learners.
8. **Appropriateness of the Figures/Diagrams:** Figures/Diagrams should be large, clear enough and proportionate in size to convey the ideas easily. Coloured chalks should be used for differentiating the various parts of the diagram and drawing the pupil's attention towards the subject matter. Use pointer if it is needed to explain the content written on the blackboard.
9. **Cleaning of Black Board**: Teacher should clean the blackboard from top to bottom and not spread dust in the classroom. He should rub the points on the black board after the student notes them down. After completion of the

lesson, the teacher should clean the entire blackboard before leaving the classroom.

Precautions while practicing the skill of blackboard writing.

In addition to above mentioned components, the student-teachers should keep in mind the following things while using the blackboard in the class.

- While using blackboard a teacher writes something on it and simultaneously speaks same words orally. Thus, the students have to use two senses viz. eye and ear at a time which makes the learning easy and effective.
- The blackboard should be well polished and smooth. Chalks of different colours may be used to make the writing and drawing attractive, clear and effective. But, white chalk should be preferred for general use.
- Be rapid in writing and drawing diagrams on the blackboard. The teacher should always be cautious to avoid writing of incorrect things on the blackboard.
- Proper margin should be given in both sides of the blackboard. The habit of writing unnecessary details on the blackboard should be avoided. Do not crowd the blackboard with written work.
- The blackboard should not be used in the manner that the teacher goes on writing and students go on copying.
- The written matter or diagram should not be removed at once. Students should be given some time to visualize and properly note down the written material on blackboard in their notebooks.

4.4.11 - Skill of achieving closure

Achieving closure is a crucial ability, much like introducing something. It's simple to introduce a subject or class, but it can occasionally be difficult to provide a strong conclusion. Instructors need to make sure they wrap up a subject methodically and understandably. Instructors need to offer just enough homework to their pupils so that they are not overburdened and can effectively retain the material.

- Questions and statements by the teacher related to the consolidation of the major points covered during the lesson
- Opportunities provided by the teacher to the pupils for linking the present knowledge with the past knowledge.
- Opportunities provided by the teacher to the pupils for applying the knowledge gained during the lesson to the new situations.

The components of the Skill of Achieving Closure are:

1) **Consolidation of major points**. Synthesizing the main points with or without the learner's involvement.
   - synthesizing the main points into a whole.
   - consolidate the main points with or without the learner's involvement.
   - Approach used by teacher may include 1) by questioning 2) by statements 3) by diagram.
2) **Providing opportunities to pupils to apply present knowledge to various new situations**

   – enable the learner to apply the acquired knowledge in various situations.

   -Feedback can be received by oral or written test.
3) **Linking past knowledge to present knowledge -what they have learned**

   – creating situations where the learners can make use of what they have learnt during
   the lesson

   – both the teacher and student can know whether or not the students have understood
   what has been taught during the lesson.

   – involves testing situations where both the learner and the teacher receive feedback
   Immediately.

   – teacher may use non-verbal media like diagrams, maps, charts.

4) Linking present knowledge to future learning

– teacher should give homework or assignment.

Assignment should be

a- most of the students can do it correctly

b- suited to the maturity level of students

c- provides opportunity to apply the present knowledge in new situation.

d-demand the application of higher mental process rather than mere recalling of previous knowledge.

4.5- Simulated Teaching.

Teacher training is crucial for the professional development of educators, providing them with the knowledge, skills, and confidence needed to be effective in the classroom. Here are some key reasons why teacher training is important to teachers:

1. Mastery of Subject Matter

- **Deep Knowledge**: Training helps teachers gain a comprehensive understanding of the subjects they teach, ensuring they can effectively convey complex concepts to students.
- **Curriculum Development**: Teachers learn how to design and implement curriculum that aligns with educational standards and student needs.

2. Effective Teaching Strategies

- **Pedagogical Skills**: Training introduces teachers to various teaching methodologies and instructional strategies, enabling them to engage students and facilitate learning.
- **Differentiated Instruction**: Teachers learn to adapt their teaching methods to accommodate diverse learning styles and abilities, ensuring all students can succeed.

3. Classroom Management

- **Behavioral Techniques**: Training provides strategies for managing classroom behavior, creating a positive learning environment, and minimizing disruptions.

- **Conflict Resolution**: Teachers develop skills to handle conflicts effectively, promoting a respectful and cooperative classroom atmosphere.

4. Assessment and Evaluation

- **Assessment Methods**: Teachers learn to use formative and summative assessments to measure student learning and progress accurately.
- **Data-Driven Instruction**: Training helps teachers interpret assessment data to inform their teaching practices and tailor instruction to meet students' needs.

5. Educational Technology

- **Integration of Technology**: Teachers become proficient in using digital tools and resources to enhance teaching and learning.
- **E-Learning Skills**: Training prepares teachers to design and implement online and blended learning experiences, adapting to modern educational environments.

6. Professional Growth and Confidence

- **Continuous Learning**: Ongoing professional development encourages teachers to stay updated with the latest educational research and innovations.
- **Self-Confidence**: Comprehensive training builds teachers' confidence in their abilities, reducing anxiety and improving their performance in the classroom.

7. Adaptability and Resilience

- **Coping with Challenges**: Training equips teachers with strategies to handle various classroom challenges, from diverse student needs to unexpected disruptions.
- **Flexibility**: Teachers learn to adapt their teaching methods and materials to different educational contexts and evolving standards.

8. Enhanced Student Outcomes

- **Improved Student Learning**: Well-trained teachers are more effective in delivering high-quality education, leading to better student performance and achievement.

- **Positive Impact**: Teachers who are confident and competent can create a more engaging and supportive learning environment, positively impacting students' attitudes towards learning.

9. Career Advancement

- **Professional Credentials**: Completing training programs and obtaining certifications can open up opportunities for career advancement and specialization.
- **Leadership Skills**: Training often includes components on leadership and mentorship, preparing teachers for roles such as department heads, instructional coaches, or administrators.

10. Job Satisfaction

- **Fulfillment**: Effective training helps teachers feel more competent and successful in their roles, leading to higher job satisfaction.
- **Support Network**: Training programs often provide opportunities to connect with other educators, fostering a sense of community and support.

Conclusion

Teacher training is essential for empowering educators with the tools and knowledge they need to succeed. It enhances their teaching effectiveness, improves classroom management, and ultimately leads to better student outcomes. By investing in comprehensive teacher training, educators can achieve professional growth, job satisfaction, and a positive impact on their students' lives.

Meaning of simulated teaching

- Simulation is a controlled representation of reality. Simulation means role- playing or rehearsal in which the process of teaching is carried out artificially. Simulated teaching is a teacher training technique. It is used to bring about modification in the behavior of the teacher. It introduces pupil teacher to teach in non-stressful conditions.

- Simulated teaching is used prior to the classroom teaching practice with the objective of developing a specific skill of communication. It can be used for pre-service teachers to make them effective.
- In simulated teaching, one pupil-teacher acts as a teacher and other teacher trainers act as students. The teacher in this situation teaches considering the student as school students.

Simulated teaching involves creating realistic teaching scenarios where teachers can practice and refine their skills without the immediate pressure of a real classroom. This can be done through:

1. **Microteaching**: Small teaching sessions where teachers present to a small group of peers or students and receive feedback.
2. **Role-Playing**: Acting out classroom situations to practice responses to various teaching challenges.
3. **Teaching Simulators**: Computer-based simulations that mimic classroom environments and student behaviors.
4. **Virtual Reality (VR)**: Immersive environments where teachers can interact with virtual students and practice teaching in a controlled setting.

4.5.1-Objectives of Simulated Teaching

Simulated teaching, also known as microteaching or mock teaching, involves practicing teaching in a controlled environment to improve teaching skills and techniques. The objectives of simulated teaching include:

1. **Skill Development**: Enhancing specific teaching skills such as lesson planning, classroom management, questioning techniques, and effective communication.
2. **Confidence Building**: Providing a safe environment for teachers to practice and gain confidence before teaching in real classrooms.
3. **Feedback and Reflection**: Allowing teachers to receive constructive feedback from peers and supervisors and reflect on their teaching practices.

4. **Experimentation and Innovation**: Enabling teachers to try out new teaching methods and strategies without the pressure of a real classroom setting.
5. **Improving Instructional Strategies**: Fine-tuning instructional strategies to meet diverse student needs and learning styles.
6. **Understanding Student Dynamics**: Gaining insights into student behaviors and learning dynamics in a simulated setting.
7. **Professional Growth**: Supporting continuous professional development and growth through practice and reflection.
8. **Assessment and Evaluation**: Providing opportunities for self-assessment and peer evaluation to identify areas for improvement.

Simulated teaching serves as a bridge between theoretical knowledge and practical application, helping teachers develop the skills and confidence needed for effective classroom instruction.

4.5.2 Educational Uses of Simulation.

Simulated teaching, also known as microteaching or mock teaching, involves practicing teaching in a controlled environment to improve teaching skills and techniques. The objectives of simulated teaching include:

1. **Skill Development**: Enhancing specific teaching skills such as lesson planning, classroom management, questioning techniques, and effective communication.
2. **Confidence Building**: Providing a safe environment for teachers to practice and gain confidence before teaching in real classrooms.
3. **Feedback and Reflection**: Allowing teachers to receive constructive feedback from peers and supervisors and reflect on their teaching practices.
4. **Experimentation and Innovation**: Enabling teachers to try out new teaching methods and strategies without the pressure of a real classroom setting.

5. **Improving Instructional Strategies**: Fine-tuning instructional strategies to meet diverse student needs and learning styles.
6. **Understanding Student Dynamics**: Gaining insights into student behaviors and learning dynamics in a simulated setting.
7. **Professional Growth**: Supporting continuous professional development and growth through practice and reflection.
8. **Assessment and Evaluation**: Providing opportunities for self-assessment and peer evaluation to identify areas for improvement.

Simulated teaching serves as a bridge between theoretical knowledge and practical application, helping teachers develop the skills and confidence needed for effective classroom instruction.

Basic Assumption

(1) Teacher behavior is modifiable by the use of feedback device.

(2) The underlying skill of teaching can be modified and practiced.

(3) Teacher behavior can be identified.

Characteristic

(1) This technique requires very systematic planning in advance that ensures attainment of desired goals.

(2) This method is effective for the practice of teaching skills by pupil teacher.

(3) The training is provided in artificial situations. Through mock trails learns are fully trained to face real situations.

(4) Through feedback drawbacks are noted in teaching, they are pointed out along with appropriate suggestions to rectify them.

Procedure of simulated training

Following are the six steps that are usually followed in simulated teaching.

(1) Assignment of role: -

The student teachers are assigned the roles of teachers and observe. It is done on rotation basis.

(2) Deciding skill to be practiced

At this stage, the skill to be practiced is decided and planning and preparation for it are done. Each trainee selects the topic according to his interest and intelligence.

(3) Preparation of work schedule

At this stage, it is decided who will teach first and who will observe and how everyone would be teaching /observing one by one.

(4) Determining technique of observation

In this stage, the decision is taken about the type of observation technique to be adopted. It also includes which type of data is to be collected and how these data are to be intercepted.

(5) Organization of first practice session

The first practice session is started and its observations are recorded for judging the teaching behavior.

This followed by feedback and suggestions for further improvement.

(6) Alteration of procedure

The whole procedure is changed at this stage. There is a change of teacher, change of observers, change of teaching skill and change in topic to be taught. Every student is given the opportunity to play the role of teacher, a student, and a teacher.

Precaution for simulated teaching

(1) Pupils for the same subject should go for practice.

(2) Each pupil-teacher should be provided with the opportunity to play the role of teacher, student, and an observer.

(3) For practice pupil- the teacher should prepare micro-lesson plan.

(4) At the end of the session there should be a decision for diagnostic processes.

Advantage of simulated teaching

(1) It is for experiencing problem situation.

(2) This technique helps us in acquiring some classroom manners.

(3) The use of this technique enables us to study and analyze the teaching problems.

(4) Self-confidence in teaching developers through simulated teaching.

(5) This technique helps in explaining the behavior problems in the classroom and contributes to its solutions.

(6) This technique makes a person more aware of the role.

(7) It bridges the gap between theory and practice of teaching.

(8) It provides them with the reinforcement to develop various teaching skills.

Limitation of simulated teaching

(1) its use cannot be made in all subjects of the curriculum.

(2) This method requires a lot of preparation on the part of the teachers which they might not be ready to take.

(3) The observer who is doing the role, may incorrectly read.

(4) For beginners, it may be difficult to practice a few teaching skills such as questioning,

(5) No emphasis is given to teaching the content.

4.5.3 Teacher Training and Simulated Teaching.

Integration in Teacher Training

Integrating simulated teaching into teacher training programs can enhance the learning experience by providing hands-on practice and immediate application of theoretical knowledge. It allows for a more comprehensive and practical approach to teacher preparation, ensuring that educators are well-prepared for the complexities of the classroom.

Conclusion

Both teacher training and simulated teaching are essential for developing effective educators. By combining theoretical knowledge with practical, simulated experiences, teacher training programs can better prepare teachers to meet the diverse needs of their students and adapt to the ever-changing educational landscape.

References

1. Ackermann E. (1996). Tools for Teaching, The World Wide Web and a web browser.
2. Agarwal, J.C.: Educational Technology and Management, Agra: Vinod Pustak Mandir. 2003.
3. Agarwal, Vibhuti. (2006). Virtual Collections in Digital Librarian, Rajat Publications, New Delhi.
4. Akdeniz, C. (2016). Instructional process and concepts in theory and practice. Singapore: Springer
5. Chand, Tara & Patel, R.N. (1992): Educational Technology, Anmol Publication, 4378/4B, Ansari Road, New Delhi - 110002.
6. Dr. Sudha, Kasireddy, Educational Technology, Sri Venkateswara University, Tirupati, Andhra
7. IGNOU, *Concept and Scope of Educational Technology,* IGNOU, New Delhi.
8. IGNOU, Education Technology B.Ed. Study Materials, New Delhi
9. Leith, G. O. et al., 1966: *A Handbook of Programmed Learning,* University of Birmingham, United Kingdom.
10. Mangal, S. K., &Mangal, U., 2017: *Essentials of Educational Technology*, PHI Learning Private Limited, Delhi. National Open University, New Delhi
11. NCERT, 2006: *Position Paper, National Focus Group on Educational Technology*, NCERT, New Delhi. Pradesh
12. S.K. Mangal: Educational Technology, P.H.I. Learning.
13. Student Teachers' Handbook for Bachelor of Education, School of Education, Indira Gandhi
14. Yogesh Kumar Singh: Basic Premise of Educational Technology.

Web resources

- http://www.gcoekmr.org/pdf/BEdCourseCode203_Unit3.pdf
- https://ddceutkal.ac.in/Syllabus/MA_Education/Paper-4.pdf
- https://concept-of-educational-technology-dr-arock.pdf
- www.wikipedia.com/teaching

- www.wikipedia/educational_technology
- https://gyanshalatips.in/the-skill-of-writing-instructional-objectives-in-behavioural-terms/
- https://yoursmartclass.com/selection-of-textbook-b-ed-notes/
- https://yoursmartclass.com/criteria-of-good-teaching/
- https://www.egyankosh.ac.in/bitstream/123456789/46590/1/Unit-8.pdf
- https://sadbhavnapublications.org/subjects.php?id=1&cid=7

www.ingramcontent.com/pod-product-compliance
Lightning Source LLC
LaVergne TN
LVHW021153160826
845679LV00024B/2099

* 9 7 9 8 8 9 4 9 8 5 2 3 7 *